DUKE OF EDINBURGH'S ROYAL REGIMENT

(BERKSHIRE AND WILTSHIRE)

1st Battalion
The Duke of Edinburgh's
Royal Regiment
(Berkshire & Wiltshire)

In 1988 The County
Infantry Battalion of
Berkshire & Wiltshire
moves to Hong Kong
for two years

WILL YOU BE THERE?

DUKE OF EDINBURGH'S ROYAL REGIMENT
(BERKSHIRE AND WILTSHIRE)

MARTIN McINTYRE

TEMPUS

Frontispiece: A poster from the late 1980s. The regiment was constantly seeking ways to gain recruits from the counties of Berkshire and Wiltshire. The designers of this poster felt that the chance to go to Hong Kong was likely to attract the right kind of men. Although these initiatives were worthwhile, it was always considered that the best recruiting aid was the soldier who persuaded his mate to join up.

First published 2007

Tempus Publishing Limited
The Mill, Brimscombe Port,
Stroud, Gloucestershire, GL5 2QG
www.tempus-publishing.com

British Library Cataloguing in Publication Data.
A catalogue record for this book is available from the British Library.

ISBN 978 0 7524 4178 8

Typesetting and origination by Tempus Publishing Limited.
Printed in Great Britain.

Contents

Above left: The cap badge worn by the regiment on its formation in 1959 was that of the Wessex Brigade. The badge had been in use since 1958 by the Royal Berkshire and Wiltshire Regiments which formed part of that brigade. It was worn until November 1969. The badge was anodised gilt for other ranks up to the rank of colour sergeant with a white metal version for officers and warrant officers class one and two. The badge is backed with the 'Brandywine flash'. This was inherited from the Royal Berkshire Regiment and was worn throughout the life of the regiment. The flash was carried over to the Royal Gloucestershire, Berkshire and Wiltshire Regiment in 1994. It will cease being worn in 2007 when a further amalgamation makes that regiment part of 'The Rifles'. (The 'Brandywine flash' was worn by the Royal Berkshire Regiment to commemorate the action of the light company of the 49th Foot during the Battle of Paoli in 1777 during the American War of Independence.)

Above right: In 1969 the Wessex Brigade was incorporated into the Prince of Wales's Division and a decision was made that regiments could revert to their former cap badges. As the regiment did not have one, it adopted the collar badge worn at that time. The silver cross pattée, which comprises the base and overall form of the badge, came from the Wiltshire Regiment cap badge. The Chinese dragon at the centre of the badge was the cap badge of the Royal Berkshire Regiment. The naval coil of rope, which was surmounted by the ducal coronet of the Colonel-in-Chief, commemorated the service of the former regiments as marines. The Brandywine flash as shown was worn on the beret only. When the regiment was stationed in Osnabrück in 1978 a small-scale experiment was tried with an all-cloth version. This was quickly discarded.

Introduction and Acknowledgements

The Duke of Edinburgh's Royal Regiment (Berkshire and Wiltshire) was formed on 9 June 1959 when the 1st Battalion Royal Berkshire Regiment (Princess Charlotte of Wales's) and the 1st Battalion Wiltshire Regiment (Duke of Edinburgh's) were amalgamated. Throughout this book The Duke of Edinburgh's Royal Regiment will be referred to as 1 DERR.

In October the same year the regiment moved to Tidworth. In June 1961 they were the first British infantry unit to train in Canada on exercise 'Pond Jump' and because of the high standards achieved they were nicknamed 'The Wonders', which came from the regimental title '1 DERR'. Another nickname acquired over the years was 'Farmer's Boys', derived from the title of the regimental march.

After Tidworth the battalion went to Malta. This was an historic occasion as they were the last unit to leave the United Kingdom in the troopship *Oxfordshire*. From Malta they trained in Libya, Tripolitania, Cyrenaica and Sardinia. In addition, the battalion deployed to Cyprus in 1964 when disorder broke out between the Greek and Turkish Cypriots. Later, each of the three rifle companies went back to Cyprus in turn to support the 1st Battalion Gloucestershire Regiment in the Sovereign Base of Episkopi. After leaving Malta they went to Minden in West Germany where they were deployed as a mechanised battalion of the 11th Infantry Brigade, in the British Army of the Rhine (BAOR). The regiment returned to Germany twice more, in 1971 (Berlin) and 1978 (Osnabrück). Following service in Minden the battalion went to Catterick, Yorkshire, where it dispatched companies worldwide: to British Honduras (now Belize) in Central America, Malaysia and to Canada for a return visit. In August 1969 'C' Company were deployed to Londonderry in support of 1st Battalion Queen's Regiment, starting an involvement with Northern Ireland that was to last for the remainder of 1 DERR's existence.

During its lifetime the battalion served throughout the world both as a unit and as sub-units as far afield as British Guiana, The Bahamas, Hong Kong, New Zealand, Hawaii, France and Norway. There were further deployments to Cyprus, one of which was as part of the United Nations Force. In 1984 the battalion was accorded the honour of providing the Queen's Guard at Buckingham Palace and in the same year was deployed during the firemen's strike and during the cruise missile demonstrations at Greenham Common in Berkshire.

During the regiment's service it greatly valued its history and traditions. Every year, when operations allowed, a parade was held as near as possible to 21 December to commemorate the Battle of Ferozeshah 1845. Due to the numbers of officers that became casualties in that battle the sergeants of the 62nd (Wiltshire) Regiment commanded companies, a fact remembered by the handing over of the Colours by the officers to the sergeants for the day at the parade, with the Colours being returned at midnight.

On formation the Battalion was part of the Wessex Brigade, later becoming part of the Prince of Wales's Division, but as a single battalion was always vulnerable when defence cuts were mooted. The regiment's final posting to England was as part the 24th Airmobile Brigade in 1990 where it received the news of the proposed merger with the Gloucestershire Regiment. This merger took place in 1994 to form the Royal Gloucestershire, Berkshire and Wiltshire Regiment (1 RGBW). In 2005 a wide-ranging re-organisation of the whole of the infantry arm of the British army was announced, under which 1 RGBW became the Royal Gloucestershire, Berkshire and Wiltshire Light Infantry to prepare them for an eventual move to the Light Division. In 2007 a further merger with the Devon and Dorsets (LI) to form the 1st Battalion of 'The Rifles' will take place, with the Royal Green Jackets and the Light Infantry forming the other four battalions.

During the life of 1 DERR there was no direct link with a territorial battalion that carried the same name. There were cross-border company links through the 1st and 2nd Battalions of the Wessex Regiment (TA), and it was to these battalions that officers and non-commissioned officers from the regiment were seconded. Because of a lack of a direct named link the territorial aspect forms no part of this book.

The style and presentation of this book has been dictated by the quantity and quality of images available. The photographs have been selected to give as wide a coverage as possible of the regiment's activities, both on active service and at rest. It is, however, restricted at times by the availability of photographs. Every effort has been made to achieve equal coverage of different generations and situations; but this has not been an easy task as, despite the many hundreds of photographs to choose from, some events were not recorded and images of events during active service are scarce. The captions are subsidiary and are intended to place the pictures in context, providing details of circumstances, dates and, where known, regimental characters. I hope this book conveys throughout a sense of the family spirit of the Duke of Edinburgh's Royal Regiment (Berkshire and Wiltshire), and also the continuity of families serving in the regiment, generation after generation. It is this spirit that has been such a great source of tenacity during the regiment's existence. It continued after the amalgamation into the Royal Gloucestershire, Berkshire and Wiltshire Regiment and even when a further merger into 'The Rifles' takes place, the spirit of 'The Farmer's Boys' will live on.

This is not intended to be a history of the regiment, but rather a selection of pictures deposited over many years. It also includes images from private collections, with many never having been published before. The official regimental history, *Cold War Warriors*, produced in 1998 by a former commanding officer, Lt.-Col. D.J.A. Stone, covers the regiment's history and deployments in detail.

Following the merger of the Royal Berkshire and Wiltshire Regiment, their two separate museums in Reading and Devizes were eventually closed and the collections united at a new location in the Cathedral Close, Salisbury, Wiltshire, in the building called 'The Wardrobe', where one of the best infantry military museums in the country has developed and is continuing to grow. The great majority of photographs in this volume are held there and are reproduced with the permission of the Museum Trustees.

Thanks are also due to: The Royal Berkshire Regiment project group (Ian Cull, Len Webb & John Chapman); Col Colin Parslow; Lt-Col (rtd) John Venus; Lt-Col (rtd) D.J.A. Stone; ex-drummers Harry Angier and John Callcut; Colin Snee; The McIntyre brothers; 'Spud' Tait; Vic Hole; Jeff Giggs; Chris Ward; Pat Glover; Dave Weaving; Derek Dowdell; Chris Giddy; 'Zoomer' Davis; Amy Rigg, Nicola Guy and the Tempus team; museum volunteers Richard Long-Fox for the superb research he has carried out on the photographic archives; Sue Johnson for her 'eagle' eye and attention to detail; ex-regimental museum curator John Peters for all the regimental advice and guidance given; Lt-Col (rtd) David Chilton, the regimental museum curator, whose continuing support in allowing me free and unlettered access to the Regimental archives has allowed this project to move forward; and last but not least, thanks to my wife Carola whose support and patience allowed me the time to complete this project.

M. McIntyre
The Royal Gloucestershire, Berkshire and Wiltshire Regiment Museum (Salisbury)
The Wardrobe, 58 The Close, Salisbury, SP1 2EX
Tel. 01722 419419
www.thewardrobe.org.uk

one

Early Days

The Duke of Edinburgh's Royal Regiment (Berkshire and Wiltshire) was formed on 9 June 1959 by an amalgamation of the Royal Berkshire Regiment (Princess Charlotte of Wales's) and the Wiltshire Regiment (Duke of Edinburgh's). The parade took place at Albany Barracks on the Isle of Wight, bringing together two regiments from neighbouring counties. The former regiments had often fought alongside each other, culminating in operations in Cyprus during the EOKA campaign. The Colours were presented by the Duke of Edinburgh, the Colonel-in-Chief, beginning an association with the regiment that was to last until it merged with the Gloucestershire Regiment in 1994.

No.1 Guard marches onto the parade square at Albany Barracks at the start of the presentation of Colours to the newly formed regiment. The 'Advance' was sounded and the guards, under command of their officers, marched on parade to the tune 'Blue Bonnets'. All of those who took part in the parade wore No.1 Dress. The march 'Blue Bonnets o'er the Border' came from the Wiltshire Regiment which had inherited it from the 99th Foot whose version of the opening lines read, 'March Past o'er the border, Some of 'em drunk, and some of 'em sober'. This tune was to become familiar to generations of soldiers who served in the ranks of 1 DERR. The officers to the right are (from the front): Lt J. Hyslop, Maj. D. Savill and 2nd-Lt A. Cole.

The new Colours are removed from the piled drums preparatory to the Colonel-in-Chief, the Duke of Edinburgh, presenting them to the regiment. He made a speech which was answered by the Commanding Officer Lt-Col G.F. Woolnough, MC, in the following terms:

> These Colours replace those of the two regiments whose traditions and history we combine on amalgamation. The honours borne on these Colours will be a reminder to us of the duty and the service we inherit from these regiments. That duty and service to our sovereign and to our country we now carry forward in the name of your regiment whose title we are honoured and proud to bear.

The new Colours carried thirty-six Battle Honours on the Queen's Colour, and twenty-seven on the Regimental Colour.

After the consecration of the new Colours, Lt J. Morris received the Queen's Colour from the Colonel-in-Chief. Lt J. Shears (hidden) has yet to receive the Regimental Colour. To the right are the piled battalion drums traditionally used to provide an altar when holding religious services in the field. Today the practice primarily occurs during the presentation of Colours. The six side drums are placed in a circle with the emblazoning the right way up, facing outwards. The bass drum is laid on the side drums and a tenor drum on top.

Above: After the Colours were presented the new battalion marched past in quick-time. This was followed by the advance in Review Order and a Royal Salute. Here we see the battalion marching past their new Colonel-in-Chief. Many of the soldiers on parade were national servicemen with recent service in Cyprus against EOKA terrorists. Watching them were numerous old soldiers from the former regiments, some with service going back to the Boer War. One such was Chelsea pensioner Thomas Alder who joined the Royal Berkshires in 1895 and fought in South Africa and France in the First World War. Another spectator was ex-Pte Weaver of the Royal Berkshire Regiment who had been paralysed by terrorist actions in Cyprus only a short time before. The battalion are marching past to the Regimental March 'The Farmer's Boy'. At the conclusion of the parade the battalion marched off the parade to the regimental march of the Royal Berkshire Regiment, 'The Dashing White Sergeant'.

Below: At the end of the parade the Colour party marched off with the new Colours. Left: Lt Morris with the Queen's Colour. Centre: Col.-Sgt Barrow. Right: Lt Shears, Regimental Colour. The two escorts were Col.-Sgts Hollingsworth and Young. The Colour party was commanded by the regiment's first Regimental Sergeant Major, Les Hodges who was also the last RSM of the Royal Berkshire Regiment. Col.-Sgt Barrow later became the fourth RSM of 1 DERR in 1966. These Colours were carried until 1984. They were eventually laid up in Salisbury Cathedral where they can be seen today.

The first photograph of the officers of 1 DERR taken at Albany Barracks, Isle of Wight, after the amalgamation parade, 9 June 1959. From left to right, back row: Lts J. Macmillan, D. Reid, G. Porter (RAEC), C. Rendle, J. Greenaway; 2nd-Lts R. Mathews, J. Kerwood; Lt A. Rose; Lt (QM) R. Tomkins; 2nd-Lts C. Boswell, A. Ravenhill, T. Millbank; Capts J. Hartland, J. Hyslop; 2nd-Lt G. Devlin. Centre Row: Lt J. Morris; Capts B. Hobbs, J. Ward; 2nd-Lts A. Larkman, R. Goodhart, A. Forbes; Capt. C. Edwards; Lt G. Nash; 2nd-Lts D. Jones, D. Thomas; Capt. W. Turner; 2nd-Lt W. Mackereth; Lt M. Draper; 2nd-Lt A. Cole; Capt. (QM) J. Harrowing; Lt H. Canning; Capt. R. Welsh; Lt C. Aylin; Capt. R. Waymouth; Lt J. Shears. Seated: Majs (QM) C. Barber, A. Fraser, R. Hunter MBE, F. Boshell, DSO MBE; Lt-Col G. Woolnough MC; Maj.-Gen. B. Coad, CB, CBE, DSO (Colonel of the Regiment); Field Marshal HRH Prince Philip, Duke of Edinburgh, KH, KT, CBE (Colonel-in-Chief); Brig. D. Hogg CBE; Lt-Col R. Bromhead MBE; Majs. R. Ward MC, D. Savill, R. Davis, F. Stone, L. Higgens (RAPC), R. Allnutt (RAPC). All of these officers came from either the Royal Berkshire or Wiltshire Regiments with the exception of Lt Millbank who we believe was the first true DERR officer.

The battalion's first permanent base after the amalgamation was at Jellalabad Barracks, Tidworth in Wiltshire. Here it initially formed part of the 1st Guards Brigade Group, 3rd Division. Many exercises were carried out to enable the battalion to work up to operational effectiveness. Here we see soldiers of the 1st Battalion under the command of a sergeant advancing up a ravine during one of these exercises; this exercise was filmed and later used as a training aid. They are dressed in the new combat suits and wearing cap comforters. The sergeant is armed with a Sterling sub machine gun and the remainder are armed with the Self Loading Rifle. (It was from Jellalabad Barracks in 1914 that the 1st Battalion Wiltshire Regiment mobilised for the First World War.)

After the amalgamation the depot at Devizes in Wiltshire continued to be used to train the overspill of recruits from the Wessex Brigade depot in Devon. Although national service was still in operation its end was in sight and the regiment embarked on a recruiting exercise throughout the two counties. Here we see the float that took first prize at the Pewsey carnival in 1960, with the Mayor of Pewsey being shown the self loading rifle. This recruiting team was led by 2nd-Lt Matthews.

A group of regular recruits of No.43 platoon destined for 1 DERR, Topsham Barracks, Exeter, November 1960. This was the last platoon of regular soldiers to train with national servicemen. From left to right, standing: Ptes Gower, Emm, Hatt, -?-, Simpson, -?-, Davis, Instan. From left to right, kneeling: Ptes Bowack (potential officer), Pankhurst, Ede. Pte Simpson was joining his brother who was already serving in the battalion. During the training this group were deployed to Exmouth after serious flooding. There they spent two days waist deep in water assisting civilians in clearing up operations together with the commandos from Lympstone. On arrival at the battalion in Tidworth the recruits were posted to 'B' Company which had just arrived back from the Bahamas.

In June 1960 'B' Company was sent to Nassau from Tidworth in support of the Royal Hampshire Regiment. It was a peaceful time carrying out a number of ceremonial functions; the only excitement was being deployed to outlying areas and islands to assist the local population after the devastating hurricane 'Donna'. Here we see a quarter guard being inspected by Brigadier Lister, the commander of the Caribbean Area, at Nassau. The company was based at Oakes Field, Nassau. Sgt R. Allcock is the guard commander who after returning to Tidworth was posted to the King's African Rifles. (Oakes Field was named after Sir Harry Oakes, reputedly the

richest man in Canada, who was murdered in Nassau in 1943. During 'B' Company's stay they were looked after by his son, Sydney Oakes, 2nd Baronet, who served in the Royal Berkshire Regiment as a national service officer at Hildesheim after the Second World War.)

Men of the 1st Battalion on exercise 'Starlight' on the main road between Tobruk and Derna, Libya, North Africa. They arrived in Libya in March 1960 having flown in Britannia aircraft from RAF Lyneham, Wiltshire, to El Adem. They carried out a number of tactical exercises over a total of 90 miles of desert. The exercise finished at El Gubba, 40 miles south-west of Derna. The ground covered during this exercise would have been familiar to the 8th Army who had fought over it seventeen years previously. (The section commander on the right is L/Cpl Dudman.)

In April 1961 the battalion took part in a large air-mobility exercise in Norfolk called 'Spring Fever'. This included internal security exercises around the villages of Stanford and Tottington. At the time any threat from civil disobedience was very much seen as Middle-East based, hence the use of pyjamas in lieu of Arab dress. Here we see three members of the battalion, having exhausted the possibilities of words, resorting to a physical solution.

During exercise 'Spring Fever' the battalion worked closely with the Norfolk constabulary. Shown here is a civilian police dog handler supported by armed guards from the battalion and covered by a Light Machine Gun post in a sandbagged emplacement. Little did these soldiers know that only three years later the battalion would practise these skills for real in Cyprus, and later still, in 1969, embark on a thirty-year on and off commitment in Ulster.

In 1961 the Battalion took part in exercise 'Pond Jump' in Canada, the first British Army unit to do so. A total of 689 from all ranks flew from RAF Lyneham to Fredericton, New Brunswick, where they exercised with the Canadian army for a period of six weeks. The battalion's advance party was met by the regimental band of the Black Watch (Royal Highland Regiment) of Canada playing 'The Farmer's Boy'.

Shortly after their arrival in Canada the battalion took part in a military tournament. Teams were selected by Brigade Headquarters, from the nominal roll of all units, with the battalion entering teams in the forced march, physical fitness, road rally, driving rodeo and first-aid competition. The battalion won outright the forced march and physical fitness section, for which the regimental journal justly reported 'much credit is due to the guts of the men who achieved this almost immediately after stepping off the plane'. Here we see Lt Spence receiving the trophy from Maj.-Gen. M. Bogart. Lt Spence later became the Regimental Secretary of the Royal Gloucestershire, Berkshire and Wiltshire Regiment.

'B' Company Anti-Tank section in a Canadian jeep with a 106mm recoilless rifle, Canada, 1961. From left to right: Ptes Bowles, Sear, Hatt, L/Cpl Wright. At the time each rifle company had support weapons such as mortars and anti tank guns attached. This was changed when the battalion went to West Germany as part of the British Army of the Rhine (BAOR) in 1965 when the support company was formed. (The battalion had the loan of two of these weapons from the Canadian Army.)

'B' Company, Anti-Tank section, firing the 106mm recoilless rifle on the ranges in Canada, this time under the command of Cpl Gigg. These weapons packed a considerable punch so the gunners took into account the back blast, the result of which can be seen in this photograph. Most of these gunners, like their counterparts in the Mortar section, suffered from premature deafness later in life. (The last time the regiment used this weapon on live operations was when the Anti-Tank platoon of the Royal Berkshire Regiment deployed on the Suez landing in 1956.)

Above: The area of Water Street, Georgetown, British Guiana, after serious rioting, February 1962. It was into this area that 'A' Company 1 DERR was sent as reinforcements for the resident battalion, the Royal Hampshire Regiment, as part of operation Windsor 2. Initially the company, together with the Royal Hampshires, mounted a stand-by force in Georgetown whilst men of the East Anglian Regiment patrolled the rural areas. The rioting (called 'Black Friday'), which cost several lives and caused damage that ran into millions of pounds, followed the calling of a general strike in protest against Dr Cheddi Jagan's austerity budget. The company deployed four days after the main riot, carrying out patrols and road blocks. The situation eased but the troops remained until April to ensure stability. Patrols to local villages provided much needed reassurance. British action was required because of considerable unease in the USA who were less than keen to have another Cuba on their doorstep.

Below: As the situation in British Guiana returned to normality, patrols from 'A' Company went into the local villages. Here we see Cpl Seaward (with baby) and Pte Chenery, engaged in a 'hearts and minds' exercise in the Amerindian village. A local Guianese girl, when interviewed in the press, said, 'What is good to see is the way they like children and the kindness with which they treat them. For dancing the twist and the rock and roll they are good – but when it comes to a foxtrot or a waltz – watch your toes'. Pte Chenery later went to Malta with the battalion. He was buried there following his death in a tragic accident.

Col.-Sgt Murdoch, 'A' Company in St Cuthbert's Ameridian village, during the 'hearts and minds' phase of the operation in British Guiana. As a colour sergeant he was responsible for re-supplying and to some extent feeding the outlying patrols. Here he is doing what generations of British soldiers excel at: communication with the local youngsters. He holds a monkey to break the ice, later distributing milk, bread and sweets. (Col.-Sgt Murdoch on his return to the UK was photographed carrying an Indian long bow that he purchased in this village. The press dubbed him 'Sgt Robin Hood'. When the picture was published in the newspapers a landlord in a Plymouth public house remarked on the resemblance between the photograph and one of his regular customers. As a result Col.-Sgt Murdoch was reunited with his twin brother who he believed had been killed in a bombing raid on Plymouth during the Blitz.)

After the situation stabilised soldiers were encouraged to see the sights in Georgetown. Here three unarmed members of 'A' Company chat to a local. This was also an excellent way to see if there were indicators of possible future disturbances. Trips were arranged locally, visiting places such as the diamond factory and Peter d'Aguiar's brewery. The company alcoholics were delighted to find the local rum at 160 per cent proof. Despite this friendly approach a platoon was always on stand-by for anti-riot duties and all the requirements of internal security such as patrolling, guards, road blocks and urban patrols were constantly needed. The company returned to Tidworth in April 1962. This deployment together with others was to stand the battalion in good stead for the future.

In December 1962 the regiment embarked on HMT *Oxfordshire* at Southampton for Malta where it was to spend the next three years. Before leaving a set of tiger and panther skins for the Corps of Drums was presented by the High Commissioner for India. This gift was in recognition of The Royal Berkshire and Wiltshire Regiments' past connection with India. The initial approach was made by ex-RSM Hodges, the regiment's first regimental sergeant major. Here we see the High Commissioner with the colonel of the Regiment, Maj.-Gen. Coad, on board the *Oxfordshire* prior to departure, inspecting the drummers wearing the new skins.

HMT *Oxfordshire*, pictured in the Grand Harbour, Malta, after disembarking the 1st Battalion and their families. In all it took three days to complete the disembarkation. The regiment's home for the next three years was St Patrick's Barracks. This was the last regular trooping voyage to leave the shores of England for foreign climes. 1 DERR relieved the Royal Highland Fusiliers who were the last unit to return on a troopship to England. (The *Oxfordshire* first carried troops in February 1957, to Singapore. Managed and run for the Ministry of Transport by the Bibby Line, she completed twenty-seven trooping voyages.)

A
PLACE
IN THE
SUN?

Travel to Malta

WITH

THE DUKE OF EDINBURGH'S
ROYAL REGIMENT

Enquire at
any army information office

Left: The regiment was one of two garrisoned on the island of Malta, GC, at this time. A 'sunshine posting' was considered to be an excellent inducement for potential regular recruits. On arrival in Malta and for most of the tour many of the battalion's soldiers were national servicemen who after training had been drafted to whichever unit required reinforcements. Those who signed up as regular soldiers normally had a choice of which regiment they went to, many opting to follow family members. Whilst in Malta, national service ended, with those already serving gradually leaving as their time expired. Regiments then had to apply more effort to regular recruitment. Specialist teams were based in England, but it was generally considered that those serving were the best recruiters. Here we see one of the early posters produced whilst the battalion was in Malta.

In 1963, 100 territorial soldiers of the 52nd (Lowland) Division flew to Malta for a three-day exercise. The objective of this deployment was to prove how quickly the Division could muster a composite company to be rushed to any trouble spot abroad. The 1st Battalion acted as the host unit, training the Scotsmen in the latest internal security duties. They also took part in an 'anti gun-running' exercise on the island of Gozo. Here we see two members of 1 DERR being taken 'prisoner' from a hastily constructed sangar (rock-built emplacement) by one of the part-time soldiers.

Right: Lt Cates (left) briefs soldiers of 1 Platoon, 'A' Company during the exercise to test the territorial soldiers. Although a staged photograph this image gives a clear view of the equipment worn at that time. The soldier in the centre is carrying an A41 man-pack radio used at platoon level. Left of the photograph is Cpl Joe Hunt who had joined the battalion from the Gloucestershire Regiment. Lt Cates later served in Cyprus with the battalion and later transferred to the Royal Army Pay Corps. The Wessex Brigade cap badge with the Brandywine backing is just visible.

Opposite below: Shortly after arriving in Malta the battalion took part in exercise 'Run Ashore'. Here we see soldiers from 'B' and 'C' companies at Mellieha Bay having been landed from the LST (Landing Ship Tank) HMS *Striker*. Most of these soldiers at this time were national servicemen. The soldier in the centre is carrying a 3.5 rocket launcher, for use against tanks. Left of the photograph is Pte Mike 'James' Bond who had a twin brother in the regiment.

The band and drums practise on the square in St Patrick's Barracks, Malta. It was essential for the musicians and drummers to keep their musical skills at the highest level. They performed on most of the parades that took place on the island including the Independence Day Parade at which the regiment's Colonel-in-Chief, the Duke of Edinburgh, represented Her Majesty the Queen. Here the buglers are carrying fifes in their left hands. On all parades they would wear the white dress uniforms officially known as No.3 dress.

The Corps of Drums lead the battalion onto the parade square at St Patrick's Barracks on one of the three Ferozeshah parades held on the island during their stay. The drummers paid great attention to their turnout and drill as they were always at the forefront of any parade. All drummers were operational soldiers, carrying out many tasks but mainly being deployed as a machine gun platoon when required.

The battalion's band and drums led by Drum Major Ford head a guard of honour down Kingsway, Valletta, to take up position for the opening of Parliament by His Excellency the Governor, October 1963. The drummers are wearing the tiger and panther skins presented to them on HMT *Oxfordshire*. (One of 1 DERR's forming regiments, the Royal Berkshire Regiment, had very strong connections to the island of Malta. It was from the island, as the 49th Foot, that they embarked for the Crimea in 1854. They were stationed on Malta on various occasions between 1882 and 1893, embarking several times for active service in Egypt, where after the battle of Tofrek in 1885, they were awarded the title 'Royal'. For the regiment, Tofrek was a unique Battle Honour and was carried on the Colours of 1 DERR.)

In November 1963 three officers and thirty-seven soldiers from the 1st Battalion took part in the Tibesti Mountains (North Africa) expedition. It was commanded by Maj. Knight with Lt Mackereth as the navigation officer. The expedition was designed to test both men and equipment in harsh desert conditions. They were re-supplied by air and eventually covered a total of 2,700 miles. Over 100 punctures were mended and, apart from major breakdowns, some 150 motor vehicle repairs were carried out. Whilst on this expedition they were informed that the president of the United States, John F. Kennedy had been assassinated. As one member later recalled 'We certainly remembered where we were when Kennedy got shot, being stuck in the desert sticks in my mind'. The team arrived back in Malta on LST *Empire Guillemot*. Here we see the expedition returning to St Patrick's Barracks behind the band and Corps of Drums led by Drum Major Ford. (Lt Mackereth later commanded the battalion in 1982 and also became the Colonel of the regiment in 1990.)

A rifle company in white dress uniforms execute an 'eyes right' as they march past the saluting dais during the independence day parade at the Floriana parade ground, Malta, 20 September 1964. Close attention would be paid to the beat of the bass drum as they concentrated on keeping the ranks straight as they marched past. Maj. P. Freeland commanded the battalion's contingent and Lt A. Searle and 2nd-Lt N. Sutton carried the Colours. (Lt Sutton later died in Northern Ireland when a Saracen Armoured personnel carrier he was commanding overturned.) A soldier from 'C' Company later remembered, 'We carried out quite a few parades in Malta, I didn't mind as we normally had the remainder of the day to ourselves, I normally ended up down the Gut' (Strait Street, nicknamed 'The Gut' by the British servicemen).

The royal Guard of Honour for Malta's Independence Celebrations, 20 September 1964. His Royal Highness, Prince Philip the Duke of Edinburgh, visited the battalion during the day, and the same guard took part in the main parade that evening at Floriana. The guard consisted of seventy-nine hand-picked soldiers under the command of Captain M. Draper. Here we see the Guard of Honour presenting arms, with the Queen's Colour lowered at the front. (The lowering or 'vailing' of Colours as part of a salute is very ancient. Sir John Smith wrote in 1591, 'If a King or great Prince passeth by, the Ensigne is to vaile his Colours close to the ground with his knee bending, in token of allegiance and submission'. This was officially recognised in Army regulations in 1799 and has been carried through to the present day.)

Malta, *c.*1963. A publicity photograph showing several members of the battalion relaxing and having a drink in the Barraca gardens, Valletta. Walking out in uniform was not unusual at that time and when civilian clothes were allowed it was normal to wear a tie. The soldier seated on the right is wearing short puttees and dark blue hose tops. It was from Malta in 1964 that a composite platoon under Lt Newton went to Italy to appear in a Rank Organisation film *The High Bright Sun* starring Dirk Bogarde and George Chakaris about the EOKA days in Cyprus. This 'expedition' was called exercise 'Sophia Loren'.

'B' Company on the ranges at Golden Bay, Malta, around 1965, firing the self-loading 7.62 rifle from the kneeling position as part of a classification shoot. All of these infantry soldiers were required to classify every year. This event was considered to be very important as these men were 'shooting for their pay'. It was from these range days that regimental shooting team members were selected. The area seen in the photograph is now occupied by a hotel.

In 1964 the battalion was put on stand-by to go to Cyprus due to the increase in inter-communal violence between the Greek and Turkish Cypriots. Here we see soldiers from 'B' Company practising their riot drills in Golden Bay camp, prior to that deployment. The primitive wire shields and wooden batons were the only items of equipment to master. The drills, although new to some of these soldiers, were well known to the older soldiers of the battalion who had carried them out when deployed in Cyprus with the former regiments in the late 1950s.

Another view of the same training, this time a snatch squad exercise. Good training, command and control were of the utmost importance to avoid soldiers being separated or losing control during live situations and thus placing themselves or their comrades in unnecessary danger. These drills were practised time and again so everybody was aware of their function. On 25 January 1964 the battalion was ordered by the Ministry of Defence to be at seventy-two hours notice to move – the task, internal security duties outside Malta, probably East Africa, later confirmed as Cyprus. On 9 February 1964 the batallion departed for Cyprus on operation 'Quilt'.

Opposite below: Point 'Bravo' on the 'Green Line', Nicosia, manned by soldiers of 'C' Company. From left to right: Ptes Miller, Haynes, Brown, Cpl Gascoigne. Although they appear relaxed this was a dangerous area which the company manned for three weeks with the Greek and Turkish irregulars frequently firing at each other. Ptes Miller and Brown had a lucky escape during one of these exchanges when a Greek Cypriot firing a light machine-gun nearly hit both of them in Constantine The Great Street.

Above: The battalion's first task on arriving in Cyprus in February 1964 was to secure the perimeter of Nicosia airfield. The regimental journal recorded, 'For many in the company digging-in had a purpose for the first time and holes went down and overhead cover went up in record time'. Here we see one of 'B' Company's emplacements with Ptes Moody (left) and Downs (right) taking a rest from their labours. The battalion remained until March then went back to Malta. Rifle companies returned to the island over the next eighteen months.

Above: On taking over the 'Green Line' in Nicosia, 'B' Company was based in what the regimental journal described as 'doubtful accommodation' in the Armenian young men's club (seen here in the background). The platoons rotated, with one platoon patrolling, guarding Company Headquarters, and providing an Instant Readiness Force, and one platoon resting. Here we see men from 'B' Company in the grounds of the club queuing up to be fed. To the right is the CQMS, R. Allcock, who was responsible for this type of administration. His experience went back to Burma, Eritrea and Cyprus with the Royal Berkshire Regiment so he was well placed to guide these young soldiers.

On 18 March 1964, patrols from Company Headquarters located a Greek Cypriot armoured bulldozer on the move in the walled city in Nicosia. Whilst being followed it threw a track and was unable to move. Sgt Parsons was deployed to take intelligence photographs. After two attempts to get the photograph and with the Greek police threatening to shoot he completed his mission with the results being taken back to Headquarters 16th Parachute Brigade under whose command the battalion operated. As a result of this event the battalion 3.5 rocket launcher teams were deployed.

Above: Cpl Davis at the 'B' Company observation point overlooking Ledra Street (otherwise known as Murder Mile), Cyprus. He is armed with a 3.5 rocket launcher issued to these posts as defence against possible armoured threats as discovered by the earlier patrols. Fortunately they were never required. This was the company's last day in this position prior to handing over to the Canadian Black Watch who were taking over as part of the United Nations peace-keeping force.

Opposite below: On arrival in Cyprus the drums platoon, together with the reconnaissance platoon, relieved a platoon of the Gloucestershire Regiment at a particularly troublesome copper mine at Havrovouni. It was here that the battalion had its first casualty, with Pte Clacher being slightly wounded by shotgun pellets discharged by a trigger-happy Cypriot. They later went into Nicosia where we see Dmr Frank being given a drink of water by a Turkish child watched by an armed Turkish policeman whilst on patrol on the 'Green Line'. The drums platoon were very much operational soldiers and were used to reinforce undermanned rifle companies. After leaving Nicosia the drums platoon went to the village of Ghaziveran where they remained until the battalion returned to Malta.

Pte Frost, armed with an SMG (sterling sub machine-gun) in the Greek Cypriot village of Mosphiler, chats with a local villager selling eggs. This was a publicity photograph but the 'hearts and minds' approach very often produced results in terms of intelligence. During its stay in Cyprus the battalion dealt with many and varied incidents. Responding to outbreaks of violence between the warring factions, road blocks, patrols and manning observation points occupied most of their time, but the experience gained by the young officers and NCOs was to stand them in good stead five years later when the Northern Ireland troubles started. The battalion returned to Malta on 3 April 1964 where its presence was required for internal security duties during the general elections and independence, both of which were then imminent. The connection to the island of Cyprus did not end there since all the rifle companies rotated back to the island, reinforcing the Glosters.

'C' Company returned to Cyprus in July 1964, remaining until September. Initially they were under the command of 1 Glosters carrying out operational tasks at Akrotiri, followed by several weeks under the command of the 3rd Battalion Green Jackets (the Rifle Brigade) at Dhekelia. Here we see Pte Thatcher of 'C' Company, on guard manning a light machine gun atop one of the vital water pumping stations, at Dhekelia in the Sovereign Base Area. (In 2007 The Green Jackets will be one of the regiments which merge with the RGBWLI to form 'The Rifles'.)

The telephone exchange known as 'Electra House' occupied by elements of Headquarters platoons, commanded by CSM Williams. Just visible on the roof is a sandbagged emplacement manned by the soldiers of the company. This building was the centre of the island's communications, and also provided an excellent vantage point overlooking the Paphos Gate police station and much of the walled city. The company had trouble from the outset when 2nd Regiment Royal Artillery left the position early, and as a result it was partially re-occupied by Greek Cypriot irregulars. After intervention by Maj. Welsh and a Greek police inspector, a compromise was reached. This was fortunate as force would have been used as a last resort to re-establish the presence.

Nicosia, (Cyprus) __23rd March , 1964.__ 196
Λευκωσία, (Κύπρος)

*M*__essrs. 1st __B__attallion, Duke of Edinburgh Royal Regiment, Nicosia__
Δοῦναι

*Δr. То :- **The Ledra Palace Hotel,***

τῷ Ξενοδοχείῳ Λήδρα Πάλας

DATE 'Ημερομηνία	PARTICULARS Λεπτομέρειαι	@	TOTAL · ΣΥΝΟΛΟΝ	
			£	Mils
	Period 2nd - 22nd March 1964.			
	12 single rooms 12 x 20 x £ 2.280		940.	—
	4 double rooms 4 x 20 x £ 4. —		320.	—
	Kitchen Amenities 20 x £ 5.—		100.	—
	Ball Room Amenities 20 x £ 3.—		60.	—
	Telephone Calls		72.	291
	— Including Press Room —		£ 1.492.	291
	(One thousand, four hundred and ninety-two pounds, 291 Mils.)			

E. & O. E.   LEDRA   PALACE
Ε. Λ. Π.   ΛΗΔΡΑ   ΠΑΛΑΣ

Manager - Διευθυντής

On taking over from the Royal Artillery in Nicosia the rifle companies were deployed in a number of locations, some comfortable, others not so. Battalion headquarters were accommodated in the Ledra Palace hotel for a period of twenty days. Observations by soldiers from the rifle companies about this arrangement are 'unprintable'. On vacating the hotel Capt. Draper was presented by the manager with a bill for £1,492. Being somewhat short of immediate funds, Capt. Draper passed the bill on to a higher authority. He never did find out if it was paid!

A 3in mortar detachment of 'B' Company dug in at Tarhuna, Libya, North Africa, 1963. Each mortar required a crew of three, with a section of mortars controlled and directed by a Mortar Fire Controller. Membership of the mortar platoon was considered to be an honour, until they were required to man-pack the equipment. From left to right: Ptes Wheaton, Downs, Emm. In later years many of these men suffered from premature deafness because at this time there were no ear defenders.

Two members of a platoon headquarters section of 'B' Company during an advance-to-contact exercise in the Libyan Desert, c.1963. The soldier in the front is carrying a 2in mortar, and the soldier to the rear is carrying a 3.5 rocket launcher (anti-tank weapon). At the end of this exercise the commanding officer Lt-Col Boshell said, 'It confirmed what I already knew – that the battalion is extremely fit, and if we had to go into action tomorrow, I would not mind leading this battalion', which was praise indeed from an officer who had fought with the Royal Berkshires in Burma during the Second World War, being awarded the DSO and Mentioned in Dispatches twice.

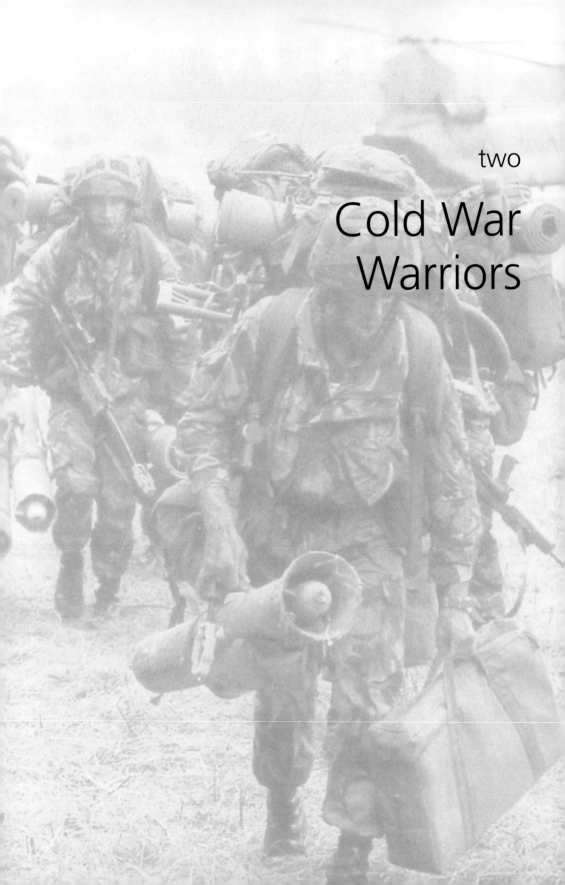

two

Cold War
Warriors

In a very cold February 1966, after three years in sunny Malta, the 1st Battalion re-formed in Minden, West Germany, as a mechanised infantry battalion in 11 Infantry Brigade – part of the British Army of the Rhine (BAOR). It was stationed in Clifton Barracks, an old Wehrmacht barracks used by the German Army during the Second World War. Here we see armoured personnel carriers and other vehicles drawn up on the parade square under the command of Lt-Col T.A. Gibson. This photograph was taken in 1969 to commemorate the tenth anniversary of the formation of the regiment. (Lt-Col Gibson previously served in the Wiltshire Regiment and was a regimental historian who wrote a number of books including the history of the Wiltshire Regiment in the Famous Regiments series.)

A general purpose machine gun team, 'A' Coy, 1st Battalion, around 1968, believed to be at the Sennelager training area during a live firing exercise. The soldier with the binoculars would be watching for the fall of shot to assist the gunner. The gunner is Pte Jock Pete, who later became the longest serving private soldier in the battalion. Just visible on his right upper arm is the 11th Infantry Brigade Flash (yellow axe). In spite of the advent of modern equipment the old skills of trench digging were still required. Most mechanised exercises involved 'digging in' on a regular basis – and, as an old soldier remembered, 'Every time it had to be filled in again'. Both these soldiers are wearing the combat caps originally issued during the Korean War. The general view among soldiers was that they were quite useless.

In 1967 the battalion took part in exercise 'Hunters Moon', held on the Sennelager training area. This exercise was conducted with US and French forces. The exercise scenario was linked directly to the need to maintain a capability to safeguard access to West Berlin. Here the battalion's armoured personnel carriers (APCs) are being readied for the exercise. Preparation was the key to success within a mechanised battalion – a point demonstrated during exercise 'Eternal Triangle' in 1966 where the battalion did not have a single case of any of its sixty-two APCs having to be sent away for second line repairs, resulting in congratulations from the divisional commander. Here we see Sgt-Maj. Dudman (left) carrying out a vehicle check with his driver with other battalion vehicles being prepared in the background.

Sgt-Maj. Whiting, in command of a 'B' Company Ferret scout car on exercise 'Hunters Moon'. The rifle company's APC 432s in the background were crewed by a driver, commander and a rifle section. They would live, work and deploy from these vehicles for the duration of any exercise. The camouflage net draped over the front would be used when the vehicles stopped for any length of time. A soldier  later remembered, 'Having served in Malta and having made many marches on foot over desert terrain, being a member of an APC crew in Germany was certainly preferable, it still wasn't easy, but it was easier on the feet'. (Sgt-Maj. Whiting had previously served in the Royal Berkshire Regiment and the Coldstream Guards.)

Above: The reality of life in a mechanised infantry battalion. Here we see a section commander together with some of his men at the garages, Clifton Barracks, Minden, around 1968. The drivers were constantly working on their vehicles. Most of the rifle sections were involved at different times, especially before any inspection (of which there were plenty). The tasks were many and varied with track maintenance being the most onerous. Most infantry battalions pride themselves on their turnout, but the effort required to keep the vehicles on the road meant that soldiers deployed to the garage area spent much of their time covered in grease. To reduce the time needed to keep kit in order the battalion ceased blancoing equipment and resorted to black boot polish shortly after arriving in Minden.

Below: Throwing a track was every APC driver's nightmare. Here we see the aftermath of such an event where the crew are contemplating the task that follows. Depending on the situation, sprockets would have to be adjusted, and bushes and pins removed from the track to enable it to be put back into working order. This would require the whole crew to assist, with the driver being the least popular member of the team. If a track was lost during an exercise where rapid movement was required the platoon commander could be one rifle section short.

Above: One of the skills required in a mechanised battalion was the ability to cross rivers in their APCs. The battalion carried out this training on the river Weser at Hameln. The drivers and commanders had to have a clear understanding of the limitations of their vehicles. A soldier from the battalion who was a driver at this time remembered, 'It was quite hairy, you were trapped in the driver's compartment attached to all sorts of wires, and received instructions from the commander who stood above you, I was very aware of the water only inches from my face on the other side of the rubber floatation screen'. Here we see an armoured vehicle from 'C' Company, with the floatation screen erected and the buoyancy tank (at the front) deployed, about to enter the river Weser. Sgt Culverhouse is second left giving instructions to the driver and Drum Maj. Morris is third from left.

Below: Having negotiated the river the next task was to exit safely on the far bank. The same soldier remembered that:

After driving into the water you had to pull hard on the tiller so you pulled the vehicle into the flow of the river, then rev the engine as hard as possible, keeping this up until you reached the far bank, remember we were blind and had to act on the commander's instructions, then the skill was to get both tracks to dig into the far bank simultaneously. If you failed a trip down the river followed, I certainly would not have liked to have done this under fire.

Here we see Sgt Simpson acting as a commander relaying instructions to the driver, carrying out such a manoeuvre. (Sgt Simpson had previous service in the Wiltshire Regiment.)

In the summer of 1971 the battalion moved to West Berlin for a two-year tour. At that time Berlin was a divided city surrounded by Communist East Germany, 100 miles from the West German border, with East Berlin directly under Soviet control. The battalion was one of three British units which made up the bulk of the Berlin Brigade. Patrolling the 'Wall' and the border with East Germany, as seen here with the Reconnaissance Platoon, was one of the main tasks of the 'Duty' battalion. Border patrols were carried out, using a Ferret scout car and Land Rover, at least twice in every twenty-four hours.

The Allied Forces Day Parade, Berlin, 13 May 1972. From left to right, standing: WO2 Brown, Maj. Morris, Pte Bolden. The Signal Platoon's vehicles under the command of Maj. Morris (Support Company Commander) drive past the saluting base. The French and Americans also took part. Other British units provided marching troops, which that year were subjected to attacks by local students with a barrage of tomatoes and eggs. After the parade many of the battalion walked up to the Olympic Stadium to watch England (under Alf Ramsey) play West Germany at football. (In 1959 it was the then Lt Morris who received the Queen's Colour from the Duke of Edinburgh on the formation of 1 DERR.)

Two soldiers from 'A' Company in a fire trench on exercise 'Quickmarch' in Schleswig-Holstein, 1971. This exercise took place whilst the battalion was based in Berlin and enabled it to practise different phases of war without the restrictions imposed within the confines of Berlin. These soldiers are manning a general purpose machine gun, set up on a tripod. Both soldiers are dressed in their nuclear, biological and chemical (NBC) warfare suits. A soldier who served at the time remembered, 'That exercise was the coldest I have ever been on; I think they even issued rum. Putting the NBC suits on was normally a bit of a pain, but on this occasion we were grateful for the extra layers to stop freezing to death.'

Sgt Murray and Pte Bridgett of 'A' Company dug in, on exercise 'Quickmarch', with an 84mm Carl Gustav anti-tank weapon, seen to the right. The regimental journal described them as 'not appearing to enjoy it'. The journal further recorded, 'Those of the administrative trail who visited 'A' and 'C' Companies paled at what they saw and returned to their Schlosses thankful that their more energetic days were over.' A further report stated that 'C' Company had a composite platoon of 3rd Company 43 Regiment of the French Army under its command. In one farm where they stayed a cat disappeared and both 'C' Company and the French suspected that the other ate it.

One of the battalion's anti-tank teams manhandle a 120mm Wombat anti-tank gun into position during exercise 'Beechnut' in La Courtine, France, 1972. Both mortars and anti-tank platoons from the battalion's support company gave fire power demonstrations to familiarise everyone with the capabilities of these weapons. The Wombat was a formidable weapon requiring a crew of three to operate it. Most of these support company soldiers were very experienced, having been in rifle companies prior to becoming either anti-tank gunners or mortar numbers. The photograph shows Pte Donahue on the left and Pte Griffin on the right. The battalion was the first British battalion to use this particular French training area since 1949.

Having manoeuvred the weapon into position the anti-tank platoon demonstrates its capability. The very important aim of these exercises was to bring home to riflemen in the companies the extent and effects of the back blast produced by the Wombat – which is evident in this photograph. The battalion's anti-tank platoon at this time was one of the best in Germany having gained over 15 per cent more hits than any other unit in BAOR in the anti-tank concentration at Putlos which took place only a month before this photograph.

In 1976 the battalion was posted to Warminster, Wiltshire, taking on the role of the demonstration battalion for the School of Infantry and the British Army. They remained at Warminster for two years, carrying out varied tasks including fire-fighting duties during the firemen's strike. Whilst in Warminster they appeared in many training films. Here we see a national newspaper advert for the army with the soldiers provided by the battalion. From left to right: Pte Brent, Cpl Snee, Ptes Carey, Shinnock, -?-, Ptes Sims, Turner. These soldiers are dressed in fighting order in front of an armoured personnel carrier (APC). After two years in this role they redeployed to Osnabrück in West Germany.

How many men are lucky enough to have 7 mates they can rely on?

Shown here is an eight-man infantry section, the Army's basic combat unit.

Eight men who live together and work together as a team.

Behind them, their Armoured Personnel Carrier, or APC for short. (All infantry sections in Germany get one.)

Every man knows his place. Every man knows what's expected of him.

Because in their book, the worst thing you can do is let your mates down by copping out.

So nobody does.

Right now, the Army needs more teams like this.

If you think you can tackle it, come and talk to us at your nearest Army Careers Information Office. (You'll find it in the telephone book under 'Army.')

Or you can post this coupon and we'll send you more facts. **The Professionals.**

I'd like to know more about soldiering. Please send me the Army's colour booklet "The Professionals".

To: Army Recruiting, MForce, P.O. Box 11, London E9 1AA.

Name .... Age next birthday ....

Address ....

ARMY

Whilst in Osnabrück the battalion went to the Suffield training area in Alberta, Canada, twice with 'A' Company visiting for a third time. Here Lt John Marsh leads heavily laden soldiers from 'B' Company during an advance over a bridge during one of the exercises. Very little had changed since the First World War in terms of weight carried by these infantrymen. The fourth soldier from the front is also carrying an 84mm Carl Gustav anti-tank weapon which in itself was a considerable weight.

In the mid-1980s controversial (nuclear) cruise missiles were delivered to the USAF base at RAF Greenham Common, Berkshire. The battalion, which had been at Howe Barracks, Canterbury, Kent, since 1983, was deployed to the base to secure it from incursions by several peace movements, especially the 'Peace Women'. The police were responsible for dealing with the demonstrators outside the fence but because of the length of the perimeter it was necessary to draft in troops to assist with the building of substantial wire fencing and watchtowers, and to also patrol them. The conditions were somewhat spartan but the troops soon adapted and made the best of it.

Here we see three soldiers from the battalion attempting to keep warm during this operation. This was the first and only time that the battalion deployed operationally within the borders of its recruiting area. From left to right: Pte Rowley, Cpl Goddard, Pte Smith. An ex-soldier of the regiment who was a member of the local police force deployed outside the wire later recalled, 'It was brilliant to see the boys again, and to see the Brandywine flash, but I don't think the lads appreciated me telling them about all the overtime I was earning, thank goodness there was a wire fence between us'. Pte Rowley served for many years and was later awarded a Mention in Dispatches in 1993. He also served at Sandhurst as an instructor. He remained in the regiment after the amalgamation with the Gloucestershire Regiment in 1994. In 2000 he became the RSM of 1 RGBW, and was later commissioned becoming the battalion's MTO.

The battalion arrived in Hong Kong in January 1988, following in the footsteps of their forebears, both of whom had served with distinction in China. The 49th Foot served in the First Opium War in 1841 which ended in the treaty of Nanking in which Hong Kong was formally ceded to the British. The China Dragon worn by the Royal Berkshires and later 1 DERR was a result of this campaign. Twenty years later the 99th Foot was part of the Anglo-French force that marched on Pekin in 1860. After the First World War the 2nd Battalion Wiltshire Regiment spent three years in Hong Kong, returning in 1929 for a year in Shanghai. They in turn were followed in 1932 by the 1st Battalion who served on active service in Shanghai during the Chinese-Japanese conflict. After the Second World War the 1st Battalion Wiltshire Regiment returned to Hong Kong garrisoning

the colony, providing drafts for Korea and manning the border. The regimental magazine *The Vly* produced this cartoon in 1987, depicting the return of the dragon.

The official ceremony to welcome the battalion to the colony, February 1988. It included a traditional Chinese lion dance, at which the Commanding Officer Lt-Col S.W.J. Saunders was asked to paint the eyes of the dragon, so giving it life for the dance, which in turn would bring good luck for the regiment. The guard of honour are still wearing No.2 Dress and have yet to be issued with the hot weather uniform. Whilst in Hong Kong the battalion was based at Stanley Fort having relieved the 2nd Battalion Coldstream Guards.

On arrival in Hong Kong the battalion took part in patrolling and manning observation posts on the Chinese border. Although most of their 'Cold War' activity to date had been against the 'Iron Curtain' and the threat posed by the Soviet bloc, the posting to the colony required the same skills overlooking what was referred to as the 'Bamboo Curtain'. Their Extensive experience from deployments in Northern Ireland meant that the operational requirements for this posting were well within the battalion's capabilities. Here we see a soldier from the battalion in one of the observation posts overlooking the border. With the Union Flag fluttering above the scene could have come from the pages of the last 200 years of the regiment's history.

The battalion went to the border region three times a year, each deployment lasting for six weeks. Based at Dills Corner training camp (used by the 1st Battalion Wiltshire Regiment in 1950) the battalion's main task was to stop illegal immigrants (otherwise known as IIs) from coming over the border. As a consequence the soldiers were armed with only batons to be used for self defence. Here we see a typical scene from one of the battalion's observation posts overlooking one of the crossing points used by the 'IIs'. In the event of a sighting one of the patrols would be directed to deal with the intruders.

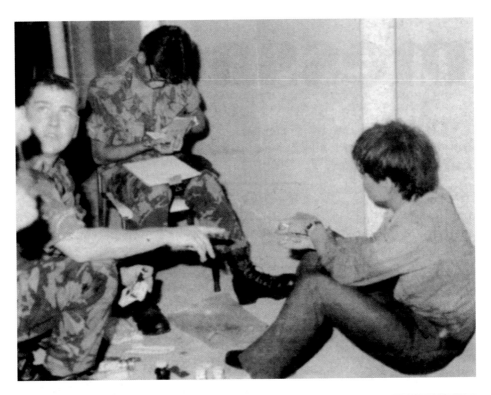

Above: Close to the border a suspected drug smuggler is questioned by Sgt Cowley of 'C' Company via an interpreter. Most of these illegal immigrants were not criminals, but this individual had a number of bottles of pills. He was handed over to the Hong Kong Police pleading his innocence, claiming he would be executed if returned to China. This type of contact was repeated many times over during the battalion's deployment on the border. Sgt Cowley's father also served in the Wiltshire Regiment and 1 DERR.

Right: Cpl Bowler and Pte O'Brien, 'A' Company, on New Bridge on the border area keeping watch for any illegal immigrants, although most of the movement took place during the hours of darkness. Both of these soldiers are carrying plastic handcuffs, the advantage being they could carry as many as they liked and they were very useful for mass arrests. They would be placed onto the prisoner's wrists, and later cut off and thrown away. They were certainly required by 'B' Company who captured fifty IIs in one night in Pak Hok Chau and Sandy Spur.

Drum Major Harrill attempts to extract the relevant information from a captured II. This prisoner has been secured with the plastic handcuffs. Once he had been handed over to the civil authorities the soldier's responsibility was finished. A soldier who served at this time remembered, 'All in all it was a bit tedious, but we still had to keep our wits about us, as although the majority of them were harmless, every now and again it was clear [that] if we were not firm, things could get out of hand'.

A good humoured international incident on the bridge at Lo Fang village. 'Passee passee' says Pte Vince Murphy as three Chinese woman try to enter Hong Kong's New Territories to work in the fields. About 2,000 trusted local people had 'tolerated' border passes issued by the Chinese authorities, but this argumentative lady did not, and was turned back. These low-level but potentially damaging contacts provided good experience for young soldiers.

By June 1990 there were 35,000 immigrants (Vietnamese boat people) incarcerated in detention camps in Hong Kong awaiting processing. As a result the battalion erected 400 tents on the Sek-Kong runway. Because it was the typhoon season they had to strike the camp a number of times. The camp was not secure, with many inmates escaping. As a consequence the battalion were required to provide a guard to safeguard MoD property. Every four weeks each company provided manpower for observation posts, patrolling the perimeter and setting up ambushes. The internal policing was left to the civil authorities. The regimental journal later recorded, 'Most of the soldiers found this a sobering and reflective experience, coming face to face with an international problem'. Here we see soldiers from the battalion putting up tents for refugees at Sek-Kong.

Shown here are soldiers from the battalion practising the riot or civil disturbance phase of exercise 'Orient Express'. After an early morning call out each company was tested in 'Cassino Village' where the rioters were provided by the 6th Gurkha Rifles. Here a shield line supported by a Saracen APC hold the cordon to allow dog units to deploy. This was familiar ground to those in the battalion who had been in Northern Ireland.

Whilst the battalion was stationed in Hong Kong it was required to provide an honour guard in Korea from 13 February 1989 for a period of ten weeks. This consisted of a platoon commander, a second in command, an admin sergeant and three sections of ten men. Based at Yong San Camp they were part of a US company, together with other units from the Philippines and Thailand. During this time they provided ceremonial guards and also tactical commitments such as guards, sentries and a quick reaction force. In May 1990 the second detachment provided two soldiers to accompany each of five coffins of returned American dead from the Korean War. This was the first such event since the end of that war. Pictured here on the left, outside the Combined Forces command building, are Sgt Long (US Army), who was the drill instructor for the UN platoon's pre-Korea training, and Cpl Cowle, a section commander.

A regimental guard of honour at the Gloster memorial in Korea 1989. From left to right: L/Cpls Travers, Evans, Ptes Trinder, Brewer, Noble and L/Cpl Stanford. Just visible on the shoulder uniforms are embroidered flashes 'Honour Guard' together with a small Union Flag. Although the British only had a token presence in Korea it was a real indication that the 'Cold War' in this area of the world was very much alive. These soldiers are presenting arms as a tribute to the men of the Gloucestershire Regiment who fell during the Korean War. Little did these soldiers realise that only five years later 1 DERR would be amalgamating with the Gloucestershire Regiment to form 1 RGBW.

In May 1991 the battalion was stationed at Catterick as part of the 24 Airmobile Brigade and was given until September of the same year to be operational in all respects. In order to achieve this, the battalion embarked on an intensive training and reorganisation programme. The aim was to be ready for a NATO exercise called 'Certain Shield'. Many new skills, concepts and doctrines had to be learned and after a significant amount of hard work, that was achieved. The main weapons system that had to be mastered was the Milan anti-tank guided missile system. In all, the battalion had thirty-eight Milan posts. From 10–18 September the battalion took part in exercise 'Certain Shield' in the area between Munster, Paderborn and Kassel in West Germany. The 24 Airmobile Brigade consisted of three infantry battalions: 1 DERR, The Green Howards (deployed as anti-tank units equipped with the Milan), and the Gloucestershire Regiment (as an airmobile infantry unit). To commemorate the regiment's role as airmobile the Regimental Band and Corps of Drums recorded a music tape.

AIRMOBILE INFANTRY

Regimental Band and Corps of Drums, 1st Battalion, THE DUKE OF EDINBURGH'S ROYAL REGIMENT (Berkshire and Wiltshire)

Heavily laden infantrymen of 'B' Company, 1 DERR, boarding a Chinook helicopter on exercise 'Certain Shield'. In addition to their bulging rucksacks and rifles they carried GPMGs (general purpose machine guns) and SF (Sustained Fire) tripods, mortar barrels, base plates and their bipods, and LAW 90s (shoulder-operated anti-tank weapons).

Milan teams move away from the Chinook helicopter after landing. The soldier at the front is carrying a Milan launcher on his back, a missile container and a bag in his hands, plus the Enfield L85A1 5.56mm assault rifle. Soldiers from their former regiments, the Royal Berkshire and Wiltshire Regiments, carried heavy loads in the First World War, as did their sons in North-West Europe and Burma in the Second World War. These, the grandsons, were carrying equally heavy loads albeit in a modern environment. It is traditional in the British Army for each generation of soldier to claim that the present generation 'has it easier' and everyone is that much softer. The reality is, although equipment and tactics may change, basic infantry soldiering remains fundamentally the same.

A 'Supacat' of 1 DERR carrying the Milan launcher, six tubular missile containers and other equipment during exercise 'Certain Shield'. The battalion had to master this and many other items of equipment. The battalion was re-organised to include an aviation company with the constant change summed up by one of the company commanders who recorded the following in the regimental journal:

1. Never believe the 'notice to move time' from your higher headquarters (it always changes).
2. Never (ever) get separated from your kit.
3. Never trust the Royal Air Force.
4. And if you don't believe that variety really is the spice of life then do not accept the job.

Soldiers of 1 DERR waiting for a helicopter prior to moving forward for an air assault on exercise 'Certain Shield'. Both soldiers to the left are carrying L4A3 GPMGs (general purpose machine gun) and Milan containerised (training) rounds. These soldiers are loaded down with enough equipment to sustain them at the landing ground and beyond. Some of these helicopter movements to the deployment area were in excess of 100km. A soldier who served at that time remembered, 'The amount of kit we carried was back-breaking, but we were very fit and it was better than 'tabbing'. ('Tab' was an army expression for 'Tactical Advance to Battle', i.e. on foot.)

Here we see a unit of 1 DERR strapped in a helicopter ready to deploy with Sgt Pocock to the right looking rather apprehensive. At the conclusion of the exercise the battalion returned to England by sea and air. In May the commander, 24 Airmobile Brigade, confirmed that the 1st Battalion had achieved the objectives set and was now 'fit-for-role' as an airmobile infantry battalion. It remained in this role until 1994 when the regiment amalgamated with the Gloucestershire Regiment.

In 1992 the battalion went to the United States for a four-week exercise 'Trumpet Dance'. The objective of this exercise was 'to confirm the operational effectiveness of 1 DERR as an airmobile battalion'. Here we see soldiers from 11 Platoon during a march and shoot competition. From left to right: Cpl Clarke, Pte Brady, Pte Redgewell, L/Cpl Noble.

Soldiers from 'D' Company 'hit the beach' during exercise 'Tofrek' at Solo Point, Fort Lewis, USA, 1992. They were landed by two US landing craft and were opposed by the local National Guard units (Territorial Army). The soldiers were using the MILES equipment which indicated whether or not a soldier was hit. In the event the equipment showed that they would have lost twelve soldiers. At the conclusion of the exercise the company made a forced march carrying all weapons and equipment to Fort Lewis. The regimental journal later reported that their American hosts were so impressed by the company's 'dash and élan' that the company commander Maj. Rylands was 'promoted' by the American hosts to the rank of honorary staff sergeant in the US National Guard.

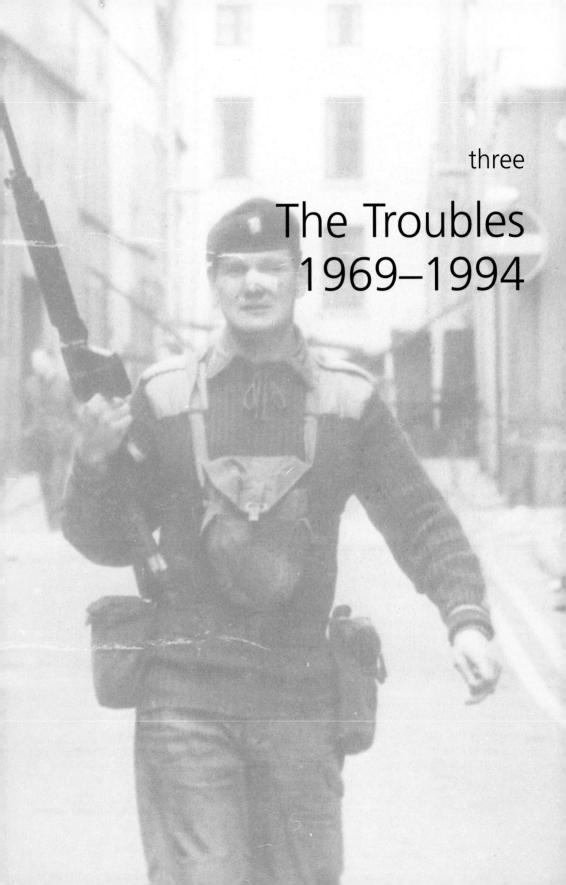

three

The Troubles
1969–1994

August 1969 saw rifle companies scattered worldwide. 'A' Company was in Malaysia, 'B' Company was in British Honduras and 'C' Company were left holding the fort at 1 DERR's base in Alma Barracks, Catterick, Yorkshire. The situation in Northern Ireland deteriorated to such a degree that extra troops were sent from the mainland. Here the commanding officer, Lt-Col T.A. Gibson addresses 'C' Company and the Drums Platoon prior to their departure. Little did these soldiers know that they were the first of several generations who would be deployed in Ulster.

'C' Company moved at short notice to Londonderry on 26 August to reinforce the 1st Battalion Queen's Regiment, remaining for four months. Here a rifle section of 9 Platoon manning a cordon to keep the warring factions apart on 24 September the same year. Behind these troops was a similar cordon facing the other way. The soldier farthest from the camera with rifle across his chest is the section commander, Cpl Wollen. Steel helmets although carried are yet to be worn and the plastic visors issued later were still in the planning stage. The remainder of the section are equipped with rifles, batons and shields. What the soldiers carried was later adjusted according to the role they were to perform.

Sgt-Maj. Parsons leads out members of 'C' Company headquarters section on the night of 24 September 1969 in Londonderry. The soldier behind him is carrying a megaphone, which was also issued to each of the platoons. The idea was to communicate if necessary with the rioting crowd; in the event they proved to be quite useless due to the noise levels in a riot situation. During this night's rioting Sgt-Maj. Parsons tried to form a protective cordon round the badly injured Mr William King who had been severely beaten. Meanwhile six soldiers were deeply engaged nearby in attempting to contain Protestants in London Street and at the same time trying to avoid the hail of missiles which rained down.

Ferryquay Street, Londonderry, 24 September 1969, a rioter is restrained by 2nd–Lt Hardwick, of 11 Platoon, as he tries to get to a senior army officer on the far side of the barbed wire. The wire is being held by Pte Wharton (nearest the shop). At the later inquest into Mr King's death 2nd–Lt Hardwick said he was threatened by several Protestants after he had grabbed a youth with a white handkerchief across his face who burst through the cordon at London Street, and hurled a bottle towards the Catholic crowd. This disturbance continued into the night requiring the troops to remain at their posts.

Pte Welsh, 11 Platoon, 'C' Company, awakens to a welcome cup of tea on the morning of 25 September 1969, in a side street in Londonderry. After the rioters had gone home the troops were required to stay in the same locations, which meant sleeping in the street. Once the situation stabilised, the troops worked nine days out on the streets, followed by three days' rest. This was repeated until the completion of the tour of duty in December. A soldier who served at that time said, 'The three days rest was a bit of a myth, the first day was spent sorting out our kit from the nine days that we had just done, the second day was rest, and the third day was preparation to go back out again'.

The same day: Cpl Fletcher, with the rest of his platoon still sleeping on the footpaths. At the inquest into the death of William King, Cpl Fletcher said, 'All hell broke loose, in the mêlée at the corner of Bishop Street and London Street where the army personnel were trying to keep back hostile Protestants from breaking into Bishop Street'. Cpl Fletcher was struck in the face when he tried to fight his way through to Mr King's aid.

Guildhall Square, Londonderry, 25 October 1969. A demonstration took place in the town to try and reinstate the disbanded 'B' Specials. The Craigavion Bridge was blocked off. The army deployed and sealed off the town in seven minutes, closing all the roads to the Bogside. Troops from the Queen's Regiment, Grenadier Guards and 'C' Company 1 DERR were involved. Here 9 Platoon, under the command of Lt D.J.A. Stone, deploy across the Guildhall Square with the Londonderry wall in the background. At the bottom right, Pte Hedges and Pte Choules make their way to the rear to assist other soldiers nearby. A soldier from this platoon later remembered:

We marched down from the Diamond in the classic square formation, behind the Queens and in front of the Guards, supported by the 17th/21st Lancers in Ferret Scout cars. As we panned out into the Square all we could do was line out with some barbed wire and push the crowd back, there were a few bricks thrown but it was over and done with fairly quickly.

(The 'B' Specials were reserve policemen who were mainly Protestant and much hated by the Catholic population.)

Above: The Diamond, Londonderry, 25 October 1969. Cpl Pavey 'encourages' locals to keep moving. This gathering was an overspill from a sit-down demonstration on the Craigavion Bridge. He is wearing the recently issued 'Flak Jacket' and wielding a wooden baton. In the small of his back is a rolled up waterproof cape. This was not for the incessant Irish rain, but as an interim measure to deal with anyone set on fire by a petrol bomb. The casualty would be wrapped in the cape to extinguish the flames. Shortly afterwards a small belt-hung fire extinguisher was issued and carried for the remainder of the tour.

Soldiers of 9 Platoon, 'C' Company, Magazine Street, Londonderry, 1969, manning the wall gate leading to the Bogside. Sketched here by artist Tony Matthews. A soldier from the platoon later remembered, 'I recollect this bloke drawing the lads, it helped with the boredom at that time, I think some of the boys posed a bit, but I might be mistaken'.

Above: An early view from the front of a 'C' Company Land Rover showing the now famous landmark on the entrance to the Bogside. When 'C' Company took up positions in this area in 1969 this wording was not in place. As the situation worsened the words 'You are now entering free Derry' were added. At this time it was the end gable of a row of dwelling houses which can just be seen in this photograph. As the troubles progressed the houses were demolished and the end gable remained, being repainted several times. This area became the focal point for many disturbances over the years.

Opposite below: An unarmed patrol of 9 Platoon in the Diamond area in the old city of Londonderry. From left to right: Pte Hiscock, Cpl Pavey, Ptes Bushell and Thomas. These were early days with the troops experimenting with different scales of equipment depending on the threat. Cpl Pavey brought his experience from serving in the 1st Wiltshires during the EOKA campaign in Cyprus, and Pte Bushell had previous experience of 'aid to the civil power' in Hong Kong whilst serving with the South Wales Borderers. He was one of many Welshmen transferred to the Regiment on the amalgamation of the South Wales Borderers and the Welch Regiment in early 1969. Although these foot patrols were unarmed, weapons were always near to hand.

Another drawing by Tony Matthews, this time showing the signaller at the headquarters of 9 Platoon, 'C' Company. During this period, when deployed the platoons took up positions throughout Londonderry in factories, disused buildings and even the jury room of the court buildings. By this time most of the platoons had their own sign board signifying who they were, with the regimental badge proudly displayed. Over the coming years each generation of 'Farmer's Boys' made their marks in similar ways.

Cpl Davis, a section commander in 10 Platoon, 'C' Company, places pickets to hold the barbed wire on one of the roads leading to the Bogside. These were very much early days and as the situation worsened and the time scales lengthened, the road blocks became more organised and permanent. Cpl Davis is wearing denim trousers, a woollen pullover and belt order, which normally consisted of a water bottle and two ammunition pouches, in which he carried one SLR magazine containing five rounds of ball ammunition, and one CS gas grenade. A soldier from the platoon later remembered, 'They didn't tell us that the gas grenades leaked after a period of time. When I used my webbing as a pillow the grenade I was carrying leaked and I got gassed whilst sleeping'.

In June 1970 'B' Company and the Drums, together with a troop from 14th Light Regiment, Royal Artillery, were dispatched at short notice to Belfast to reinforce the Royal Scots. The company commander, Maj. Godwin-Austen, later remembered, 'On the morning of the 3rd July we conducted Lord Balniel, the Defence Minister, around our company area in an atmosphere of relaxed euphoria and bonhomie. Friendly Irish neighbours gave our patrols tea and sandwiches. By nightfall we were locked in a gun battle with snipers in which at least five civilians were killed and nearly 800 rounds of 7.62 ammunition were fired by British troops.' These are believed to be members of 5 Platoon taking cover in the Falls Road.

5 Platoon, 'B' Company, Falls Road, Belfast. The violent situation started after a search of a house in Balken Street for arms and ammunition by the Royal Scots and RUC (Royal Ulster Constabulary) in which fifteen pistols, one rifle, a Schmeisser sub-machine gun and a quantity of ammunition and explosives were found. This find sparked off some of the bloodiest rioting that the province had seen to date. By the end eighteen soldiers were suffering from gunshot and grenade splinter wounds, five civilians died and 300 people were detained, and for the first time an area of Belfast had been placed under military curfew.

Above left: Maj. Godwin–Austen recalled:

On the night of 3rd/4th July 'B' Company was involved in serious rioting in the Falls Road area of Belfast, in the course of which several men were injured by gelignite bombs. In the operations that followed an officer and two soldiers of the Gloucestershire Regiment were shot and wounded. During this period 'B' Coy. expended 488 CS cartridges, sixty-four CS Grenades and several rounds of 7.62mm ball ammunition. Suddenly at the far end of the street a double-decker bus appeared. The rioters commandeered it, drove it towards us and finally placed it across the road about thirty yards in front of us. There was a pause during which we prepared to move forward to the area of the bus. Suddenly without warning, there were a series of shattering bangs in and around us. Soldiers were blown backwards, and I immediately thought we were being grenaded – and we were! All together we had seven bombs thrown at us. With this new development the platoons scattered to a tactical deployment against the walls of buildings. Eight members of 5 Platoon were injured, three having been dragged from the ranks giving a clear indication of the scale of the ferocity. The two most badly injured were Sergeant Potter and Private Fern.

This photograph shows the aftermath of the incident referred to with soldiers of 'B' Company on the left.

Above right: Sgt Potter, 5 Platoon's sergeant, received a Mention in Dispatches for his work that night, his citation reads:

During the late afternoon of 3 July 1970, the company was deployed to Albert Street, Belfast, where serious rioting was taking place. Sgt Potter was the platoon sergeant of No.5 Platoon which had been deployed at the junction of Albert Street and Raglan Street. On the arrival of the platoon, a crowd of about 400 youths pelted them with bottles, stones, ball bearings and marbles fired from catapults, and later with gelignite grenades. Sgt Potter was wounded in the hand early on in the action and suffered a fractured finger which was also badly cut. In spite of his painful injury, he continually organised and controlled repeated baton charges by his two leading sections. By his presence and calm bearing, he was able to steady the front rank under a continuous hail of missiles and bring the mission to a successful conclusion. Later in the evening, after he received attention to his wounds, he returned to the platoon and remained with them in the cordon of the Falls area for the rest of the night and the following day. Sgt Potter displayed courage and devotion to duty and contributed greatly to the success of the operations his platoon carried out during the night.

In 1971 the battalion was the 'spearhead' battalion and on stand-by for deployment anywhere in the world to protect British interests. On 22 April that year the battalion was dispatched to Londonderry, remaining until 28 May. They were based in an empty factory in Drumahoe, just outside Londonderry. Here we see 4 Platoon, 'B' Company practising their riot drills. The tactics were always being adapted depending on the latest experience. This formation, although based on the 'Box formation', has been adjusted to position those with baton rounds (rubber bullets) in the rear rank. The first two ranks are carrying short shields and batons, the third rank long shields, and the rear rank, baton guns and self loading rifles. (The metal riot shields carried by 'C' Company in 1969 were quickly discarded as being unsuitable and the shields seen in this photograph were adopted. With minor modifications they remain in service.)

During the short deployment in 1971 the battalion conducted operations in Tyrone, Fermanagh and Antrim, with 'C' Company detached for a brief period in the city of Londonderry under the command of the 2nd Parachute battalion. This tour was relatively peaceful with a few minor finds to their credit. Here we see a typical scene out in the Ulster countryside with soldiers from 'B' Company searching disused homesteads. Shortly afterwards the battalion returned to Catterick to prepare for its move to Berlin.

'Tin City', Sennelager, West Germany, 1972. The battalion had moved down to Sennelager from its Berlin station for this intensive period of training, which covered all operational possibilities needed for its forthcoming two-year posting to Ballykinler, Northern Ireland. Here we see members of 9 Platoon, 'C' Company carrying out their riot drills. To the rear is Sgt Venus who is directing the platoon's movement and speed. Carrying the baton gun is Cpl Coleman; the soldier crouching in a fire position is carrying a sniper rifle, used to cover snatch squads against potential IRA ambushes. (Cpl Coleman had previously served in the Rhodesian armed forces and the King's Own Royal Border Regiment.)

The battalion arrived in Ballykinler in July 1973, assuming operational responsibility as the Northern Ireland Province Reserve. The next two years were to be extremely busy with hazards not only confined to the IRA and terrorist action. Accidents involving heavy armoured vehicles on tracks and minor roads that were designed for light traffic were common. Here we see the aftermath of one such incident with soldiers from Lt Chilton's platoon counting their blessings after an accident with no casualties. On 14 August Capt. Sutton was not so lucky. He was returning from Portadown to Ballykinler with 'B' Company when his vehicle went out of control and rolled over crushing him. He died shortly afterwards.

In August 1973, 'C' Company were deployed to the Bogside area of Londonderry, an area very familiar to the old soldiers of this company. Here we see Sgt-Maj. Davis, the weapons training warrant officer, on the wall overlooking the Bogside. Together with the two company snipers he kept watch from this position. They utilised some tailor's dummies dressed up in army clothing. These dummies not only confused the Catholics down in the Bogside, but also fooled the Protestants up on the walls with one female schoolteacher protesting against the partially clad soldiers seen displaying themselves on the battlements.

Three of the 'C' Company snipers meet Lt-Gen. Sir Frank King, General Officer Commanding Northern Ireland, in Londonderry 1973. From left to right: Ptes Dowdell, Cook and Allen. When positioned on the wall and other locations these soldiers provided much assistance to vehicle and foot patrols whose visibility was restricted. Pte Dowdell had an older brother in 'A' Company who had served for many years, and Pte Cook's brother also served in the battalion, with their father having served in the Wiltshire Regiment. (Pte Dowdell's brother's son later joined the regiment, remaining after the amalgamation with the Gloucestershire Regiment. On 1 RGBW's tour of Bosnia he was killed together with three other soldiers from the battalion when their armoured vehicle came off a mountain road.)

A fairly typical scene in Northern Ireland. A vehicle check point near the village of Tandragee manned by soldiers of 'A' Company during the tour of 1973–75 on the occasion of the anniversary of Bloody Sunday. The objective of these checks was to stop or disrupt the IRA running bombs to Belfast. An old soldier who served on this check point remembered, 'This was a Loyalist area and the armoured vehicle you see in the photo was full of bottles of beer, whisky, cakes and sandwiches'. The soldier with the clipboard is Cpl Kew whose brother also served in the battalion. His father had served in 1 DERR and the Royal Berkshire Regiment. His grandfather, who was a pre-First World War regular soldier with the Royal Berkshire Regiment, won the DCM, MM and Bar, was commissioned and won the MC and Bar.

Ten years on, young soldiers who could well have been at school when the previous photograph was taken are engaged on the same task. This shows a vehicle check point on the Dublin Road in South Armagh in 1983, where the attitude from the locals was markedly different. Vehicle check points were considered very boring, but soldiers realised that this tactic assisted greatly in disrupting the movement of arms and explosives. Shortly after this photograph was taken soldiers from 'B' Company picked up a suspect in this area who was 'wanted for questioning'.

Above: Sgt Davis with a significant arms find made by search teams from 'A' Company at the Fire Station in Portadown, 1973. Two men, both loyalist paramilitaries, were arrested. Items found included a self-loading rifle, four revolvers, an air pistol, and 2,500 rounds of 7.62 ammunition – all stolen from the Ulster Defence Regiment. Although discoveries of this type provided a significant rise in morale, encouraging other soldiers to search more thoroughly, many man hours were expended with negative results.

Below: Graffiti in Portadown 1973, which reads 'Dukes are yellow bastards'. Although a form of abuse, it was considered to be an unofficial indicator of the battalion's success in hitting the right targets. A regimental magazine at the time reported:

Pte Iles the company clerk drew to the CSM's attention a notice on a wall in red paint ... at which point they all rushed back to camp and checked all the admin cards to make sure the next of kins were correct, this being so they heaved a sigh of relief.

Comments of this type featured on many walls throughout the province during each tour.

Opposite top: On 15 October 1974 Republican prisoners serving sentences in the Maze Prison rioted. The battalion was mobilised to deal with it, with tactical headquarters and two companies flying directly to the Maze from Ballykinler, while 'D' Company came by road from Aughnacloy in Saracen armoured personnel carriers. This was not a spontaneous outbreak of violence by the inmates but a planned event, designed to coincide with other disturbances in Northern Ireland. Here we see a Saracen APC commanded by L/Cpl Finnegan with soldiers from 'D' Company and the Drums on foot either side. A private soldier who was on the other side of the wall at this time with his platoon sergeant, Sgt Baleimatuku, remembered, 'There were three of us trapped behind the wall, we kept firing volley after volley of baton rounds until we almost ran out, it was life threatening stuff. We were rescued when 'Donkey' Finnegan came crashing through the wall with his Saracen, were we pleased to see him.'

Opposite middle, left: Here prisoners, some of whom were wearing equipment 'captured' from troops, confront 'C' Company. The prisoners were well prepared for their action; they had erected barricades, stockpiled bricks and hunks of concrete, made various weapons such as poles with 6in nails embedded in their ends, improvised maces and pieces of beds with their ends made as jagged as possible. They even had respirators. Pte Giddy remembered:

> I can't remember the exact time we went in but it was light. The company entered the Maze and we went into what looked like a sports field. It was a single gate and as we got in we panned out into what could only be described as an extended line. I was a baton gunner as were many others. To say it was a turkey shoot is no exaggeration, however poor fire discipline meant we soon ran out of rounds. When that happened the tide turned and we began a hasty withdrawal.

Opposite middle, right: 'C' Company were under extreme pressure and several soldiers were separated with their lives in immediate danger. Pte Giddy had one such experience:

> I was at the extreme flank and following the radio operator that went through the gate before me, unfortunately his webbing caught the gate which closed and I was left on the wrong side. It was pure numbers kicking each other to get to me that probably saved my life. In no time at all I had lost my webbing, helmet, FRG [Baton gun] and flak jacket. In the process I had more than a few blows to the head and other parts of the body. My head had begun to bleed where I had been hit with my own FRG, how's that for adding insult to injury. I had been stabbed in the back a few times with a make shift knife, probably a screw driver. I tried to reason with the gentlemen even telling them that my grandmother was Irish. Couldn't think of any thing else to say except don't kill me. Of course she wasn't but it was worth a try. The only thing that I could think of was to stay on my feet because if I went down I would be stamped to death. By this time a helicopter was overhead and one of the terrorists told me to wave to the crew, I think in the hope of keeping it at bay, however as soon as they saw me they dropped CS gas by the ton (well, it was probably not that much). As the gas hit the ground the mob either dispersed or went to ground I stood up and the next thing that I recall was snatch teams all over the place.

Here we see Pte Giddy's flak jacket, recovered after the riots, showing clear signs of the assault.

Opposite bottom: One of the snatch squads remove a prisoner, with the remainder of the group being lined up against the prison wall. Many soldiers from the battalion sustained minor injuries with thirteen going to Musgrove Hospital in Belfast for treatment.

Another view of the same area with soldiers removing recently searched prisoners. The inmates at the Maze were experienced men and as such operated under their own command structure inside the prison system. Prior to the disturbances the republican prisoners had a local truce with the loyalist prisoners enabling them to use some of their cell accommodation as a field hospital.

After the battle was over the prisoners (there were over 400 of them) were lined up against the wire at the edge of the football pitch, and during the day were taken back to the various compounds. By 1800 hours that evening the battalion had left the prison with the prisoners, now well and truly subdued, preparing to spend a cold night without shelter, as the regimental journal said, 'Well they did burn their own huts down didn't they'. And so ended one of the regiment's most violent episodes to date. (The estimated cost of damage to the Maze Prison, during disturbances on 15 October 1974, was put at £1.5 million.)

On 28 October 1974 a massive IRA bomb exploded outside the Sandes Soldiers Home which was situated just outside the Ballykinler barracks. At the time it was full of soldiers on their morning break. The building caught fire and collapsed. Cpl Coughlan and Pte Swanick were killed and thirty-three others were injured, some badly. In addition two civilian members of staff also died. Here we see the aftermath of the explosion with soldiers on the left giving first aid to Cpl Ron Sutton who was seriously injured. He was later medically discharged, but continued to play a significant role in Regimental Association matters.

An aerial photograph of what remained of Sandes Soldiers Home which graphically shows the extent of the damage. There were a number of reasons put forward for the attack on it by the IRA – the battalion's involvement at the Maze Prison riot, or revenge for the death of Paul Magorrian who was shot by members of the battalion in August. In either case it mattered not, the battalion continued with its task. The Home was later rebuilt and on a subsequent tour the battalion erected a monument to the two soldiers who had lost their lives there.

St Columba's School, Brandywell, Londonderry, 1973. A search team from 'A' Company with a sniffer dog after an incident at this location. It was from this position that 'A' Company observed the Bogside. The IRA became aware of this and set a booby trap for the next patrol that was due to take up a position. Before it arrived the device was accidentally set off by the school's headmaster and the caretaker. Fortunately neither were killed, but both were injured. The remnants of the caretaker's clothing are hanging in the nearby tree. The incident provided valuable lessons to young soldiers of the battalion about movement into and out of positions such as this.

Whilst on patrol near the border with Southern Ireland, and close to Cullhanna, Pte 'Chuck' Stoneham, who was carrying an A41 radio, had a lucky escape when a gunman opened fire from a nearby hill. The first round went through the radio just after he had removed it from his back. Another member of the patrol immediately raked the gunman's position with his GPMG (general purpose machine gun) giving the section commander, Cpl Gardiner, time to organise his section. Pte Stoneham was heard to roundly curse his malfunctioning radio not realising it had been hit. Reinforcements were therefore summoned by telephone. The gunmen made good their escape in a car across the border. This photograph shows the damage to the radio.

The battalion returned to Ireland in 1979 from Osnabrück, Germany. On 9, 10 and 11 August 1979 riots took place on the anniversaries of 'Troops Out', 'Apprentice Boys March' and the tenth anniversary of 'Troops in'. This scene in Sackville Street, Londonderry, was a familiar one to generations of soldiers who served in the province. 'D' Company, under the command of Maj. Parslow, confronted this crowd. Missiles were thrown and the company commander ordered the wearing of steel helmets. One young officer who was slow to act paid the price with a minor injury.

The aftermath of the riot shown above with Lt Tomlinson nursing a head wound which later required seventeen stitches. It was caused by a Coca Cola bottle bouncing off a door frame and striking the unfortunate officer. The regimental history later recorded that he received scant sympathy from his colleagues as it was quite possible he would be charged with having sustained a self inflicted injury due to his failure to get his helmet on quickly enough. In the event he wasn't and was left to the mercy of his fellow officers. (Injuries of this type were commonplace with most soldiers returning to duty fairly quickly after treatment.)

Here we see soldiers from 'D' Company, 1979, removing part of a barricade in William Street, Londonderry. They are wearing the helmets introduced in 1975; these were the new glass fibre reinforced plastic type which gave greater protection and stability. The soldier in the background, carrying the self-loading rifle, has the new helmet with visor attached. Pte Mark Reading (on the right without his helmet) is helping to remove the barricade.

August 1979, ten years after the regiment's first deployment, soldiers from the battalion move from a Land Rover to take up positions on the edge of the Bogside in Londonderry. The writing on the wall was familiar to all those who served in this city. By this time the buildings behind had been demolished leaving only the end wall. (See page 61.)

On Tuesday 28 August 1979 the band of 1 DERR were due to give a concert in Brussels. Just after the bandsmen left the temporary stage to put on their uniforms it was destroyed by a massive explosion. Two bandsmen and eleven tourists were wounded. Within minutes of the blast the Mayor of Brussels, Pierre Halterman, received a call from the IRA claiming responsibility. Bandsman Robert Finlay stated at the time, 'I was at the back of the rostrum when the bomb went off, I was bowled over by the blast and when I got up, I saw bandsmen sprawled everywhere'. Here a young bandsman inspects the wrecked instruments. At the time the battalion were on a four months' operational tour in Londonderry.

Six years earlier, in 1973, the band of 1 DERR had marched through Broad Street, Reading, Berkshire, as part of a recruiting exercise prior to the battalion's deployment to Northern Ireland. The band was followed by 100 members of the Anti-Interment League (AIL) with their banners. The AIL members picketed the local shops and handed out leaflets. The whole event was reported by the PIRA newspaper in Dublin *An Phoblacht* with headlines such as, 'Everybody laughed at the British Army'.

A patrol from 1 DERR moves through Magazine Gate leading to the Bogside, Londonderry, 1979. Front, right: the patrol commander, Cpl Tait. Left: Pte Hall. Rear, right: Pte Hillier. Cpl Tait remained in the regiment for many years, up to and including the amalgamation with the Gloucestershire Regiment in 1994. He later became the new regiment's second RSM, retiring as a captain. His brother also served in the regiment. Capt. Tait later recalled, 'I remember that photograph being taken, in fact we went through the gate several times for the photographer, we could have done without it as we were rather busy, anyway it looks like we are posing which I can assure you we were not'.

Londonderry, Northern Ireland, 1979. Cpl Colin Snee in the first of two Land Rovers returning from the Bogside after helping another patrol to safely extract itself from a difficult situation. The driver is Pte R. McIntyre and the two soldiers at the top are Ptes Barton and Kordowski. The Land Rover has its doors removed to allow quick access. At the front the 'wire cutter' post fitted above the passenger door was designed to stop soldiers who were standing in the rear compartment being decapitated by wire strung between lamp-posts. Both Cpl Snee's and Pte McIntyre's sons followed them into the regiment.

In 1983 the battalion had a very eventful tour in South Armagh. Here we see members of an incident control point manned by 'A' Company in Crossmaglen. The previous day the base had been mortared and a clearance operation was in progress. Ten minutes after this photograph was taken the derelict building in the centre of the picture blew up. An explosive charge had been set to injure those clearing up. Fortunately the only casualty was a Royal Engineer with a minor flesh wound to his leg.

The battalion returned to the province in 1985, being stationed at Aldergrove. Here we see CSM North showing the General Officer Commanding, Northern Ireland, the destruction caused by a mortar attack in Dungannon in January 1986. They are both standing at the spot where four members of 'A' Company tried to take cover under one bed. There were no serious casualties although a number of men were buried under rubble and rendered unconscious. Patrols were dispatched in order to make the area safe and CSM North later reported, 'Everyone returned to camp and the planned dinner night for the officers and their guests started after midnight'. (The response mirrored an event in Waziristan on 12 April 1924, when the Royal Berkshire Regiment (one of 1 DERR's ancestor regiments) suffered heavy sniper attack at night from local tribesmen taking advantage of bad weather. But as Lt-Col Davidson-Houston, recalled, 'We had a guest night and a concert afterwards.')

Here we see soldiers from 'B' Company deployed at Mullen Bridge in the County of Fermanagh, 1987. The conditions in locations like this could, and in some cases did, result in ailments and conditions that soldiers from an earlier age would recognise. One such ailment was 'Trench Foot'. Fortunately this was not a regular problem. Maintaining their personal equipment and weapons in the very damp Irish environment presented the soldiers with constant challenges.

On Remembrance Sunday, 8 November 1987, the IRA detonated a huge bomb alongside the War Memorial in Enniskillen killing eleven civilians and wounding hundreds more. 'B' Company, under the command of Maj. Wardle was directly involved. Maj. Wardle, who at that time together with other officers from the company was in civilian clothes, became the incident commander. He later recounted his experience in the regimental history *Cold War Warriors*, 'Moments into the incident an alert 'B' Company Lance Corporal ran up to me and handed me his radio set. 'Here Sir,' he said, 'You'll be needing this'. This photograph captured that moment, also showing the immediate carnage caused by this bomb. Two weeks later the parade took place with the Prime Minister Margaret Thatcher in attendance, Maj. Wardle was again the local incident commander.

On 17 February 1991 'D' Company together with a dog handler from 4 UDR were conducting a search in a rural area of Fermanagh. During the search an incident occurred which tested the 'veterinary skills' of the patrol when they came across a cow about to calve. They assisted in the best traditions of 'The Farmer's Boys' with the dog handler pressed into service as a vet and the remainder of the patrol, under the command of Cpl Court, protecting the scene and offering much advice. From left to right: Pte Shuttleworth, L/Cpl Leighfield, Pte Boyd (UDR), Pte Chelmis, Pte Lane.

L/Cpl Pugh and Pte Davis on patrol in Fermanagh West, 1991. These patrols varied in length from eight hours to five days with the average being about thirty-six hours. L/Cpl Pugh is armed with a light support weapon and Pte Davis with an SA 80 rifle. Good infantry skills were required to patrol these areas but soldiers were always vulnerable to sniper attacks. This was to happen two years later on the battalion's last tour in the province when two young soldiers were shot by snipers in South Armagh.

Vintage .50 calibre heavy machine guns were re-issued to units after a number of permanent vehicle check points (PVCPs) came under attack. Here we see Pte Bishop at the Mullan Bridge PVCP near the border in Fermanagh carrying one of these heavy weapons. When the Gortmullan PVCP was hit by seven rounds on 20 April 1991 Cpl Alden immediately activated the attack alarm and dropped the anti-ramming barriers. He then brought the Browning machine-gun into action, gaining his place in history as the first soldier to use this weapon in a contact in Ireland against the IRA. Sgt Rowley organised an *ad hoc* force, leaving the relative cover of the PVCP. He then began an assault towards the enemy position using fire and manoeuvre. The terrorist team withdrew into the Republic of Ireland.

Men of 'D' Company, on board a Wessex helicopter, en route to a border operation in 1991. They were based in St Angelo camp, with their operational orders covering the whole of the battalion's area. This, which included more than 100 miles of the border with the Irish Republic, totalled 726 square miles. Movement by helicopter was therefore absolutely vital. 'D' Company was the Airborne Reaction Force (ARF) for the Battalion. For incidents in the immediate area of Fermanagh the ARF was at ten minutes notice to move. The best example of the use of the force was when it supported 'B' Company as they dealt with a hoax proxy bomb at Kilturk check point. The force was on the ground in exactly the right place within minutes of 'B' Company being attacked.

In 1993 1 DERR returned to Ireland for the last time before the regiment's amalgamation. The battalion was based in South Armagh. This painted sign greeted all visitors as they got off the helicopter at Crossmaglen. During this posting this base was garrisoned by 'C' Company. This photograph was taken on 7 April, shortly after an IRA mortar attack, one of two suffered during this tour of duty. L/Cpl Overson, Pte Coleman and Pte Weston were wounded when the company came under fire during four separate shooting incidents and on 17 July 1993 Pte Pullin was murdered by the IRA.

A reconstruction of how the IRA sniper Michael Carragher fired the .50 Barrett Model 82 sniping rifle from the back of a Mazda vehicle through the aperture in the armoured-plated shield fitted in the rear. It was this weapon that killed Pte Kevin Pullin on 17 July 1993 while on foot patrol on the Carran Road in Crossmaglen. He was the third and final soldier from the regiment to lose his life in Crossmaglen (Cpl Windsor and Pte Allen died in 1974) prior to amalgamation with the Glosters. Sixteen of the twenty-four sniper attacks in South Armagh involved the use of an estate car, van or jeep acting as a mobile firing platform, clearly highlighting the problems for infantrymen patrolling or manning static check points.

Flanked by L/Cpl Lavender and Cpl Carr, Capt. Godwin (who had been the battalion's regimental sergeant major from 1989 to 1990) co-ordinates helicopter movement at Bessbrook, 1993. This heli-base was recognised as the busiest in Europe. During this tour of duty Bessbrook was the battalion's headquarters, from where they maintained three security bases at Newtonhamilton, Crossmaglen and Forkhill. It was at Newtonhamilton on 24 June 1993 that nineteen-year-old Pte Randell was shot and killed by an IRA sniper.

Ptes Charlesworth and Kelly in South Armagh, 1993, taking up a fire position to protect the area around a newly discovered bomb while it was defused. The device had been spotted by a sharp-eyed sergeant from the battalion. It was a significant find, with the device intended to be detonated by command wire with a second much larger bomb timed to explode up to forty-eight hours later in the hope of killing soldiers engaged in the follow up operation. More than 700lb of explosives were recovered. The battalion had come a long way from its first posting to the province in 1969 when it deployed with very little equipment. At the end of the tour of duty came a return to Catterick to prepare for the forthcoming amalgamation with the Gloucestershire Regiment. (The general purpose machine gun (nearest camera) had been re-issued to troops on operations to provide a heavier hitting capability.)

four

Barrack Life

Saint Patrick's Barracks, Malta. The battalion took over these barracks from the Royal Highland Fusiliers in December 1962 and remained there until 1965. From there the battalion went on active service to Cyprus in 1964, plus many exercises in North Africa (Libya) and Sardinia.

Below: The battalion heavy and light weight Tug-of-War teams, champions of Malta command, 1964, at the Marsa sports ground. From left to right, standing: Cpl Hadley (coach and trainer), Pte Wilson, Cpls Wright and Hole, Ptes Greening and Dor, L/Cpl Williams, Pte Hyde, Sgt Stafford (became RSM 1976), CSM Barrow (became RSM 1966). From left to right, kneeling: Ptes -?-, Groom, Mullen, Tull, Neville, Cpl Cripps, Pte Shears, Cpl Davis. There were very few major units on the island but the team made their mark on the first serious contest when they beat the 2nd Royal Malta Artillery (who had won the championship for seven years in succession) by two pulls to nil. These regimental sportsmen followed in the footsteps of the Royal Berkshire and Wiltshire Regiments which both fielded outstanding Tug-of-War teams.

In early 1964 the Battalion was deployed from Malta to Cyprus as a result of the deteriorating relations between the Turkish and Greek communities. Initially responsible for the defence of Nicosia Airport, they were later given the task of manning 'The Green Line' in Nicosia itself. The regimental diary recorded that 'B' Company 'was to have half the old city based on rather doubtful accommodation in the Armenian young men's club. The O.C. [Maj. Graham] returned from the reconnaissance muttering about the squalor, four hour shifts and claustrophobia'. A soldier from 'B' Company remembered, 'It was the pits'. Although the building was cleaned up most of the platoons spent the bulk of their time deployed on operations in the city. Here we see an armed sentry outside the main door of the club.

The battalion served in West Germany from 1966 to 1969, stationed in Clifton Barracks, Minden. In common with most German barracks of this type the accommodation surrounded the parade square. The sergeants' mess can be seen in the background of this photograph. Shown here is a guard of honour for the Colonel-in-Chief, The Prince Philip, Duke of Edinburgh. On the left is the guard commander, Maj. Ridley, followed by the commanding officer Lt-Col Gibson. The warrant officer in the front rank is Sgt-Maj. Parsons and the soldier nearest the camera in the rear rank, wearing the white lanyard, is Pte Dyer. This lanyard indicates that the soldier was a member of the signal platoon.

The Corps of Drums, led by acting Drum Major Cpl Venn, on the parade square, Clifton Barracks, Minden, West Germany, 1968. This photograph was taken shortly after the issuing of the new drummers' helmets, minus the helmet plates that followed a short while later. The bass drummer in the centre is Dave Smith who, after retirement, became the chairman of the RGBW Reading branch of the Regimental Association. Second row, left: Bob Safe, the tenor drummer, who was killed in a tragic accident on 9 November 1968. While carrying out maintenance on the Drums Platoon's Armoured Personnel Carriers, he was crushed to death between a vehicle and a garage wall. He was later buried in his home town of Salisbury.

The band and drums led by Drum Major Morris and Bandmaster Hibbs march through the streets of Minden, before leaving for the United Kingdom 1969. They are carrying out an old custom of 'All Debts Paid' (also known as Change of Quarters) which was the converse of 'Crying Down the Credits' when a regiment arrived in station. Traditionally drummers were used to announce to the local shop owners, alehouse keepers, and traders that the regiment was about to leave and that they should seek settlement of any unpaid bills. Local hostelries were well patronised – as a soldier who served in the battalion in Minden remembered, 'We certainly frequented the bars of that town, when not on exercise we were drinking either in the company club or the town every night' but whether any local traders took up the offer is not known.

After leaving Minden the battalion was posted to Alma Barracks, Catterick, Yorkshire. Very few of the soldiers spent more than a few months in the camp, with companies being deployed all over the world. For 'A' Company it meant swapping the comforts of the barracks for the jungle of Malaysia on exercise 'Sanjak'. Here we see one of the platoons prior to an exercise. Left to right, back row: Pte Anderson, -?-, -?-, Cpl Hicks, Pte Kendrick, -?-, Pte Sheikh. Second row: Cpl Poynter, Pte Sutton, -?-, Pte Stevens, -?-, -?-, Pte Paz, Pte Bell. Front row: L/Cpl Waite, Pte Clements, -?-, Cpl Trench, Lt Morris, Sgt -?-, L/Cpl -?-, Pte Haddow, -?-, Pte West. Cpl Hicks later became the regimental sergeant major in 1983 after which he was commissioned. His musical skills were nil so his last posting prior to retirement came as a shock – as quartermaster of the Army School of Music at Kneller Hall!

Cpl Poynter of 2 Platoon, 'A' Company, leads a patrol along a jungle path, during one of the exercises in Malaysia. He is followed by Ptes Kingsley, Sutton and Stevens. Cpl Poynter is armed with an American Armalite assault rifle, Pte Kingsley with the standard issue self-loading rifle, and Pte Sutton with the Light Machine Gun. The training in jungle tactics was very necessary because, whilst based at Alma Barracks, the battalion was rotating rifle companies through British Honduras (now Belize) in Central America for six-month tours.

In British Honduras during 1969–70, the battalion was responsible for the security of the country which was traditionally under threat from its neighbours, the Republic of Guatemala, which regarded the country as one of its provinces. The companies were based in Airport Camp not far from Belize City, but spent a significant amount of time patrolling the border areas. When in barracks at Airport Camp, ceremonial events took up part of the time. Here we see Maj. Ridley with Lord Shepherd, Secretary of State for Commonwealth Affairs, inspecting a quarter guard found by 'B' Company. The soldiers of the guard are wearing the white No.3 Dress. A soldier who served with 'B' Company remembered, 'I really enjoyed it in BH [British Honduras], although very hot we soon became acclimatised, although I never quite got used to the local booze called "Swampie", a local version of rum which tasted like paint stripper'.

As well as maintaining their own military skills, whilst in British Honduras the companies also trained the local defence forces. Here we see WO2 Leeder of 'B' Company at the passing out parade of No.2 Police Special Force Unit, 13 January 1970. The police units were in fact para-military, used not only for military duties but also as the riot squads for the colony. A soldier who served at the time remembered, 'I'm not sure how they would have fared in the military sense, but as riot police go I think they could hold their own anywhere'. (WO2 Leeder had previously served in the Royal Berkshire Regiment on active service during the EOKA campaign in Cyprus. After amalgamation he was stationed in Malta, returning to Cyprus in 1964. He also took part as an extra in the film *High Bright Sun* starring Dirk Bogarde. He served in Sardinia, Minden (BAOR) and Belfast, Northern Ireland, when 'B' Company had a short but violent introduction to the Troubles. He retired from the army after serving as the RSM at Welbeck College.)

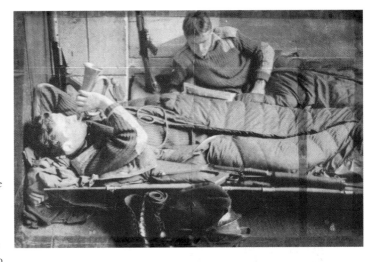

Londonderry, Northern Ireland, 1969. Barracks in those early days were disused factories, old buildings, or anywhere a platoon of troops could rest for three days prior to a further nine days 'on the street'. Here we see Drummer Lovegrove and L/Cpl Fielding. This is a publicity photograph as the platoon drummers would not have been allowed to play their instruments in such a fashion. At the time drummers were attached to each platoon. Their function was to blow bugle commands to the troops, and also to attract the attention of a crowd. At least that was the theory – experience soon showed that it did not work and it was quickly phased out with drummers deploying as rifle sections in their own right.

A group of 1 DERR Regimental Policemen, early 1980s. From left to right, back row: L/Cpl Petherick, Pte Hawkins, Pte Leaman. From left to right, sitting: Sgt Batty, Sgt-Maj. Mehrlich, Cpl Hiscock. Although barracks might change, discipline within them did not, with breaches of rules being dealt with by the Regimental Police. They always wore a black armband on the left arm with the letters RP and the regimental badge thereon. During the day they were used to round up delinquent soldiers who may have committed some real (or imagined) offence for fatigue duties. An ex-sergeant major remembered, 'It was not unknown for some RSMs to recruit soldiers who had returned from the army prison at Colchester known as "The Glasshouse" as members of the RP section, poachers turned gamekeepers as it were'. It was useful if members of this section could box. Sgt-Maj. Mehrlich was a battalion boxer of note, winning the Army Light Weight Boxing Championship in 1972. He later served with the Royal Scots in the first Gulf War and retired as a lieutenant colonel.

The battalion served in West Berlin from 1971–73 based in Brooke Barracks. Here we see a quarter guard, 1st Battalion, 29 October 1972, commanded by Sgt Venus, presenting arms on the arrival of HRH the Prince of Wales. The visit coincided with three of the Prince of Wales's Division Regiments being in Berlin at the same time. (1 Cheshire Regiment, 1 Worcestershire and Sherwood Foresters Regiment, 1 DERR). The Prince remained with the battalion for about an hour. The link between the regiment and his father was not lost on Prince Charles when he commented, 'I gather you are known as "Dad's Army"'! (Sgt Venus became the regiment's RSM in 1980 after which he was commissioned.)

On 2 May 1973 the battalion marked its departure from Berlin by staging a 'Farewell Historical Pageant' in the Kongresshalle, near the Brandenburg Gate. It consisted of a number of tableaux, one of which was the stand of the last eleven of the 66th (Berkshire) Regiment at Maiwand, Afghanistan, in 1880, by members of 'B' Company. The dog representing 'Bobbie' was a stuffed Dalmatian covered in talcum powder to hide the spots (the ruse failed). Centre with his arm in a sling is Sgt A. Hobbs, whose brother also served in the regiment. L/Cpl Wise (with his head bandaged) is kneeling to his front.

Whilst in Berlin there was an unusual duty location – Spandau Prison. Seen here in 1972, a sentry from 'B' Company, 1 DERR, mans a guard post on the corner of the prison that held only one prisoner, Rudolf Hess. The main prison wall was in turn surrounded by an electric fence with prominent warning signs to stay clear. The building to the right is the governor's residence, and also the temporary barracks for the platoon providing the guard which was rotated between the British, French, Americans and Russians. A corporal who took part in this guard duty remembered:

> We were warned not to speak to Hess, and that he would attempt to engage the sentries in conversation, after which he would immediately report the sentry to the guard commander so we kept well clear of him. It was an eerie place with only the one man inside it. Nevertheless it was an interesting duty to carry out.

A view from one of the sentry posts in Spandau Prison showing Rudolf Hess walking through his garden, around 1972. Cameras were forbidden in the sentry posts, as were cigarettes, but both managed to find their way in. Pte Suchocka later remembered:

> No.3 post is right opposite his [Hess's] quarters and he comes out every morning and afternoon for one to two hours. He walks round and round wearing paths in the grass, but not sticking to the same route. He will be walking around and then suddenly will break into a high goose-step. Sometimes he just stands below the guard post and stares up at the guard. It drives you mad, we try to ignore him but it is hard.

The battalion remained in Berlin until July 1973 before returning to Northern Ireland for two years at Ballykinler.

Left: The battalion arrived in Ballykinler in July 1973, assuming operational responsibility as the Northern Ireland Province Reserve. It remained here until January 1975, having what turned out to be one of the most active tours of the regiment's existence. The tone was set on the arrival of the advance party who were mortared. A year later the adjacent camp was IRA-mortared from a position in the centre of Ballykinler village. Here we see Capt. Pook with the IRA mortar used to attack the camp. (Capt. Pook, who was a Devonshire and Dorset Regiment officer, was the battalion's Operations Officer at the time. In 1973 he became the Northern Ireland individual orienteering champion. In 1984 he was the second in command of 1 DERR when new Colours were presented at Canterbury, and later commanded the 1st Battalion Wessex Regiment (Rifle Volunteers).)

Below: Northern Ireland, 1973. The commanding officer Lt-Col Turner (centre) with (left) Maj. Martin (R. Hampshires – attached) and (right) RSM Pinchen visit 'B' Company's location, thought to be Portadown. Maj. Martin, a military historian, later went on to command the 1st Battalion Royal Hampshire Regiment, and after retirement became a managing director of Holts Battlefield Tours. Lt-Col Turner later became the Colonel of the Regiment in 1988, remaining in post for only a short period before retiring due to ill health. Both Lt-Col Turner and RSM Pinchen had previously served in the Wiltshire Regiment during the EOKA campaign in Cyprus in the late 1950s.

Right: On 14 August 1973, Capt. N.J. Sutton died as a result of a vehicle accident in Northern Ireland. He was the second in command of 'B' Company. Returning from Portadown to Ballykinler he was commanding one of the company's Saracen armoured personnel carriers when it went out of control and rolled over. He was buried with full Military Honours at Tidworth Military Cemetery in Wiltshire. The bearer party was commanded by RSM Leadbetter. Here we see the guard reversing arms with the 'Last Post' played by Cpl Hiscock. (The sounding of the 'Last Post' at a military funeral is the deceased's 'goodbye' to this world.)

Below: Barracks for 12 Platoon (Drums), together with Cpl Searle's section of 10 Platoon, was a location known as 'The Hump' VCP (vehicle check point). This was on the border of the Republic of Ireland near the town of Strabane. In the aerial photograph below (22 February 1974), the platoon's position is just to the left of the industrial buildings near the bottom of the picture close to the bank of the river Foyle. At about 0645 hours they came under fire from IRA gunmen located at the Inter Counties Hotel (top left of the photograph). Just as Pte Stanley identified the firing point the position was hit by two mortar bombs. Pte Stanley engaged the enemy with the machine gun and was joined by Pte S. McIntyre who spotted for the gunner. Pte McIntyre then engaged the target with his rifle after the GPMG had a stoppage. Pte Harrill (who later became the drum major) and Pte Poole engaged the target while Cpls Searle and Gill attempted to rearrange the gun positions as thirty mortar bombs fell (fourteen failed to explode). The engagement lasted for forty-five minutes. Cpl Gill was later awarded the Military Medal.

To provide accommodation for the ever increasing numbers of troops, HMS *Maidstone* was brought out of mothballs and converted into temporary barracks for those based in Belfast. The battalion took up residence twice on this ship. The Drums Platoon, which was attached to 'B' Company, was the first in 1970. 'A' Company followed in 1973, when they deployed as the 39 Brigade Reserve for Belfast. Here, serving under the command of 42 Heavy Regiment, Royal Artillery, they were heavily committed in Belfast city-centre operations. They also supported the Queen's Own Hussars during a tense period of sectarian confrontation in the Lenadoon area, and, in the Falls Road area, worked with 40 Commando, Royal Marines for march control duties, and with 1 Royal Green Jackets for patrol duties.

The same problem arose with the posting to Londonderry and another old ship was used. From 11–18 July 1974 'B' Company were based on HMS *Rame Head*, an old destroyer repair ship built in 1944 in Vancouver. Anchored alongside Fort George, she was used to accommodate 350 soldiers. Whilst here 'B' Company acted as brigade reserve, mainly supporting the Grenadier Guards on the Shantallow estate. During this short deployment they were very busy and were heavily stoned on two occasions. Here we see a member of the company standing guard.

Above: During the Cyprus posting of 1975–76, the Corps of Drums, led by Drum Major Coveney, with Col.-Sgt Hobbs as second in command, were stationed at RAF Troodos as a rapid reaction force for the radar installation located nearby. In the autumn of 1975 they came across the result of a Ford Anglia failing to navigate a very sharp bend. Working for two hours in the hot sun they recovered the bodies. Third from left: Dmr Callcutt; right: Dmr Brown.

Below: As a result of this incident Col.-Sgt Hobbs was awarded the General Officer Commanding Cyprus's personal commendation for Meritorious Service. It read:

> On 22nd September 1975 the Corps of Drums, 1st Battalion, the Duke of Edinburgh's Royal Regiment were returning to Episkopi from Troodos after a tour of duty. The platoon was commanded by Col Sgt. Hobbs. Ahead of them a car drove off the road and plunged five-hundred feet to the valley below. The car contained three passengers, a man and a woman, and a child. Led by Col.-Sgt. Hobbs, the Corps of Drums climbed down the cliff face to give aid. They found that the two adults had been killed and the child so severely injured that she died soon after the accident. Col.-Sgt. Hobbs immediately organised the recovery of the bodies which had to be carried up the hill to a waiting ambulance. Throughout the operation, which was both difficult and of necessity carried out in a dignified manner, his conduct, leadership and determination were of the highest order, and his coolness and humanity made a profound impression upon the crowd who witnessed the incident. Col.-Sgt. Hobbs and the men of the Corps of Drums acted in the highest tradition of the British Army, and brought great credit to the regiment, Near East Land Forces, and the Army.

Here we see Col.-Sgt. Hobbs (now a drum major) receiving his award.

In 1977 the battalion was sent to Scotland on operation 'Burberry' to provide fire cover during the firemen's strike. They deployed to Glasgow, Lanark, Grenock, Prestwick and Kilburnie. Due to this commitment the Ferozeshah parade was cancelled and the Colonel-in-Chief, HRH the Duke of Edinburgh, who was due to take the salute, flew to Scotland to visit the troops. Here we see him with Maj. Bradley and the commanding officer, Lt-Col Jones (with glasses), watching soldiers from 'A' Company practising their fire-fighting skills. A soldier who was there at the time remembered:

It was good for morale to see the Duke of Edinburgh. In order to impress him we had to demonstrate the use of one of the Green Goddess appliances arriving at an incident. Unfortunately our inexperience showed itself when the vehicle, with a water tank only half full, failed to take a corner properly and crashed into a lamp post in front of the Duke, I think he smiled, but I'm not sure.

One of the units was based at Prestwick Airport, being accommodated at HMS *Gannet*. This team of sixty soldiers and four Green Goddesses operated mainly in Ayr, Kilmarnock, Irving and Prestwick. They remained there for five weeks tackling ninety-four fires. Here we see one of those teams at Prestwick Headquarters. From left to right, standing: Cpl Parsons, Ptes Charles, Gomersall, Driver -?- Royal Corps of Transport; sitting: Pte -?-; kneeling: Pte Alden. On every call-out each team would be accompanied by a patrol car from the Strathclyde Police.

Soldiers from the detachment at Queenslie tackle a rooftop blaze in Glasgow. In the first twelve days of operations they turned out to sixty-eight alarms, resulting in forty fires having to be extinguished. False alarms with good intent amounted to seven, and there were nine hoaxes. This was a good experience for the young soldiers, even allowing for potential local violence such as the threat offered to one of the teams after extinguishing a fire at a house when a young boy said, 'Which team do you support Rangers or Celtic? Tell me or I'll bash you'. After this deployment they returned to Battlesbury Barracks, Warminster, resuming their duties as demonstration battalion.

Apart from the first few years of the regiment's existence, when National Service was in being, it was an all-regular unit. Although soldiers joined the regiment from all over the United Kingdom, and in some cases from other parts of the world such as Fiji, the main recruiting areas were the counties of Berkshire and Wiltshire. Because the regiment was always posted abroad it was necessary to carry out recruiting exercises within the two counties called KAPE tours (Keep the Army in the Public Eye). Here we see camouflaged Land-Rovers from the support company on one such tour in June 1978 in Queen Street, Salisbury, Wiltshire, taking part in the carnival procession.

The barrack accommodation in the Masonic Camp of 9 Platoon (attached to 'A' Company), Londonderry, c.1979. By this time the conditions had improved somewhat but were still very basic and cramped. These soldiers have their equipment stored in such a way that when called out everything was to hand. This part of the barracks held twenty-four men. A sergeant who was there at the time remembered, 'It might seem cramped to you, but to us it was not a problem as they kept us out on the street most of the time'.

British Regiments have a tradition of leaving examples of their regimental badge in prominent places when on operations or based in faraway places. (Both battalions of the Wiltshires left very large rock carvings of their badges in Cherat, India, before the First World War.) Cpl Hawkins of 'B' Company, 1 DERR, was responsible for a number of these examples in Northern Ireland. Here we see him applying the finishing touches to the badge on the wall of their base during the 1979 Londonderry tour. Cpl Hawkins was later awarded the British Empire Medal for his work. In Osnabrück, West Germany, during the battalion's 1978–84 tour, he designed and refurbished the dining area of the cookhouse into a very smart convivial restaurant. At the opening it was aptly named the 'Hawkins Restaurant'.

The Corps of Drums 1981, Osnabrück, West Germany. From left to right, back row: Dmrs Hanson, Tollfield, Hamilton, Winters, R. Tollfield, Coulson, Woolford. Second row: Dmrs Adcock, Savage, Rowel, Cook, Lymon, Dartnell, Bridgewater, Scott, Callcut, Heatherwick, Preston, Margison. Front Row: Cpls Callcut, Davis, Drum Maj. Harrill, Capt. Walker, Cpl Stanley, L/Cpl Thurtell. The Drums Platoon of 1 DERR is believed to be the only Corps of Drums within the British Army which used glockenspiels, seen on either side of this photograph with banners representing the former regiments. The following year Drummer Margison was killed in a road accident.

In December 1984 the battalion commenced a six-month United Nations tour of duty in Cyprus. This was the first 'blue beret tour' carried out by the regiment since its formation. The battalion was split in two with battalion headquarters and two companies deployed to the west of Nicosia whilst the remainder were based in the Eastern Sovereign Base Area at Dhekelia. The opportunity was taken to pay respects to the soldiers from the Royal Berkshire and Wiltshire Regiments who had been killed during the EOKA campaign in the late 1950s. Here we see Maj. Nigel Walker (centre) together with Commanding Officer Lt-Col Kenway (right) while drummers from the battalion play the 'Last Post'.

The battalion went to Hong Kong in 1988 where they relieved the 2nd Battalion Coldstream Guards. They were stationed in barracks at Stanley Fort. The fort was sited on the Stanley Peninsula, at the extreme southern tip of Hong Kong island, overlooking the South China Sea. Here we see the Corps of Drums, under the command of Drum Major Harrill, with part of the barracks in the background. The regimental flag is located at the front of Battalion Headquarters.

In 1989 'D' Company, reinforced by the Drums Platoon, flew from Hong Kong to Hawaii on exercise 'Union Pacific' where they had the opportunity to train with American forces. Here we see the Drums at Schofield Barracks, Oahu, Hawaii, under the command of Sgt Smith during the American Army's 3/22 Infantry Battalions 'Organisation Day'. 'D' Company exercised with Company K, 3rd Battalion, 3rd Marines. It was reported in the Hawaii Marine Corps newspaper that Marine Lt Simonsen expressed surprise at the amount of equipment the British soldiers carried (e.g. Full MOOP-4 (Fighting order), forty-eight hours of combat rations, cooking utensils and a tent).

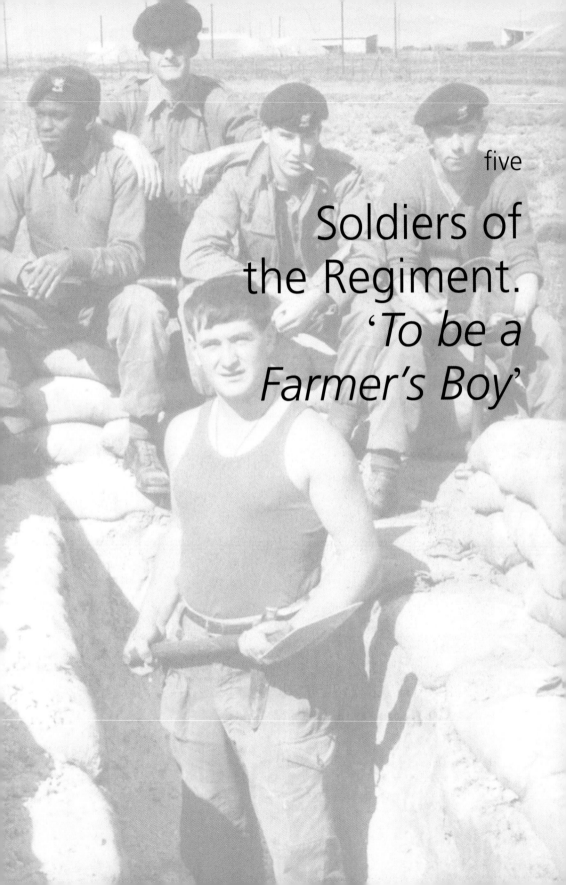

five

Soldiers of the Regiment. *'To be a Farmer's Boy'*

This print depicts the scene that relates to the words of the Regimental March 'The Farmer's Boy'. The song originated in North Oxfordshire as a folk ballad, and the tune is that of a patriotic song of the Napoleonic Wars 'Ye Sons of Albion'. The first verse reads:

The sun had set behind
yon hill,
Across the dreary moor
When weary and lame,
a boy there came,
Up to the farmer's door,
Can you tell me
whe're I be,
And one that will me
employ?
Chorus:
To plough and sow, to
reap and mow,
And be a farmer's boy,
and be a farmer's boy.

Officers and sergeants had to know the whole song by heart, on pain of extra duties, and many soldiers who served fondly remember the march being sung with gusto in different parts of the world as a prelude to robust activity against an opposing regiment. 1 DERR was a family regiment with son following father and with many groups of brothers serving, all of whom referred to themselves as 'Farmer's Boys'.

No.1 Platoon, 'A' Company at the end of exercise 'Dragons Teeth' at Schleswig-Holstein, 7 November 1972, prior to returning to Berlin. Led by Cpl Sutton (centre) the soldiers are giving a good rendering of the regimental march. Pte Spraggon is nearest the camera. Cpl Sutton was later seriously injured in the Sandes Soldiers Home explosion in Ballykinler, Northern Ireland, the following year when two members of the regiment were killed.

During its time in Malta, 1962–65, the battalion took full advantage of the sporting facilities, participating in football, hockey and cross country running at the highest levels. Here we see the officers' rowing team, Malta, 1965. In the officers' race they were narrowly beaten by the King's Own Malta Regiment. Despite many hours of hard training, the team never came first. From left to right, back row: Capt. Wadham, Capt. Jones (commanding officer 1977), Capt. Sammons, Capt. Mackereth (CO 1982, colonel of the Regiment 1990). Front Row: Capt. Vernon-Powell, Lt (QM) Smyth, BEM, Lt A. Kenway. Captains Vernon-Powell and Mackereth both became qualified helicopter pilots. Capt. Vernon-Powell had a long association with the Army Air Corps, later becoming CO 9 AAC. Lt Kenway subsequently served for a period with the Special Air Service and, on becoming commanding officer of 1 DERR in 1984, placed great store on personal fitness.

In 1964 the battalion deployed from Malta to Cyprus on operation 'Quilt'. The first task was to secure the perimeter of Nicosia Airport. Here we see soldiers from 'B' Company taking a rest from their labours whilst digging in on the perimeter which at that time was thought to be vulnerable to attack by Turkish forces. From left to right: Ptes Onuaguluchi, Leahy, Cooper and Harper, with Pte McGlyn standing in the trench. Pte Leahy, a battalion boxer, and later a regimental policeman, was killed by IRA action in Northern Ireland in 1973. Pte Cooper (holding a hunting knife) later joined the Royal Air Force rising through the ranks to group captain. Pte Onuaguluchi, after returning to Nigeria, became the marketing manager of the Agricultural Development Corporation in Enugu.

Pte Rowe (left) and CSM Barrow on the 'Green Line' separating the Greek and Turkish communities in Nicosia, Cyprus, 1964. Both these soldiers had come from Malta as part of the reinforcements for the Cyprus garrison. CSM Barrow had previously served on the island with the 1st Battalion Wiltshire Regiment against the EOKA terrorists. He was a member of the Wiltshires' search team in 1958 that was responsible for the death of the EOKA second-in-command,

Christoforou Matsis. He had a great enthusiasm for the Corps of Drums and recognised the need to preserve the customs, traditions and music, hitherto handed down by word of mouth, in a more permanent form. This culminated in the production of *The Drummer's Handbook* with musical content provided by WO2 Hall of the Coldstream Guards, a publication still in use today.

Cpl Povey on duty at a sandbagged observation point in Cyprus 1964 overlooking the 'Green Line', the neutral zone one street in width, separating the Greek and Turkish communities. Cpl Povey started his army service in the Royal Berkshire Regiment just prior to the amalgamation. He spent the remainder of his service with 1 DERR, retiring as a sergeant major. After retirement he maintained strong links with the regiment as an active member of the Regimental Association. Following the amalgamation with the Gloucestershire Regiment in 1994 he subsequently became a member of the association executive looking after the interests of retired members of the regiment.

Opposite above: In 1964, 'A' Company was attached to the 1st Battalion Gloucestershire Regiment in Cyprus. In December that year the company commemorated the Battle of Ferozeshah. Here we see that parade being inspected. From left to right: Maj. Stone, WO2 (CSM) Williams, Cpl Hawkes, Lt-Col Radice (Commanding Officer of 1 Glosters), Cpl Cawley, L/Cpls Venus, Cummings, -?-, Pte Scully (Rear rank with glasses). WO2 Williams later became the fifth RSM of the regiment and L/Cpl Venus the tenth. This photograph is of interest as it was taken at the time when the battalion was changing from the old battle dress, as worn by the guard to the new No.2 Dress as worn by Cpl Hawkes.

Above: 'A' Company, 1 DERR, jungle training, Malaysia, on exercise 'Sanjak', 1969. Brigadier Grey (General Staff HQ Singapore District) meets with Lt Mawle (Centre) and the company commander, Maj. Lea-Cox. Lt Mawle was the commander of 1 Platoon and was responsible for leading the successful battalion Cambrian March team to second place in 1969. Whilst in the battalion he was prominent in rugby, shooting and orienteering. He later joined the Dhafa Gendarmerie and was killed on 10 October 1971. Maj. Lea-Cox had previously served in the Wiltshire Regiment and became 1 DERR's eighth commanding officer in 1975. He had already seen active service in the Congo whilst serving the Ghanaian army 1959–60, and was later awarded a Mention in Dispatches for his work in Northern Ireland.

Both the Royal Berkshire and Wiltshire Regiments were very much family regiments and this was carried over into 1 DERR with many pairs of brothers serving. Here we see some of those in the 1st Battalion in 1969 in Minden, West Germany. From left to right: Dando, Stockley, Sillence, White, Browne, Choules, Potter, Collins, Watton, Watson, Barnfield, Cook, Sawyer, Hiscock, Iles. (Not present: Burton, Edmonds, Jordan, Maher, Dowdell.) The high numbers of brothers serving in the battalion continued right up until the amalgamation in 1994, and beyond into 1 RGBW.

The Minty family provided six generations of soldiers for the 62nd, Wiltshire Regiment and 1 DERR. Here we see three at the passing out parade for the youngest member at the Lichfield Depot in 1988. From left to right: Capt. P. King, RSM N. Minty, Pte J. Minty, Brigadier Hargreave, CBE, ex-Sgt A. Minty, RSM Turner. (The family line went back to 1839 when a great-great-great-grandfather served as a canteen sergeant in the 62nd. Another member served in the Wiltshire Militia, with a third serving from 1906 to 1929 when he died in Shanghai. Ex-Sgt A. Minty served from 1937 to 1957. RSM Minty joined 1 DERR in 1964, serving until retiring as a lieutenant colonel in 2005. His son joined the regiment in 1988.)

Soldiers from 5 Platoon, 'B' Company, come out of the trenches while on exercise 'Quick March' in Schleswig–Holstein, 1971. This area was used by the Berlin Brigade because of a lack of training space in Berlin. The weather on this exercise was extremely cold and good discipline was needed to maintain standards. A soldier who served in this platoon remembered, 'It was freezing, but they still kept us in the trenches, I suppose it was good training. I remember the photo being taken, we were brought out of the trench line to get paid, then we went back with nowhere to spend it. It proves that someone at battalion headquarters had a sense of humour'. These soldiers are all wearing the 'caps combat' that were not held in great esteem. This group is led by Sgt Johnson, followed by Cpl Pinnell Cpl M. McIntyre and Pte Collins. Cpl McIntyre was the eldest of five brothers who were to serve in the regiment up to and including the amalgamation in 1994.

A group of solders serving in the battalion in Hong Kong, 1988, after being presented with their awards for service in Northern Ireland. From left to right: Capt. Barlow (MBE), Sgt A. Gill (MID), Col.-Sgt B. McIntyre (MID), Lt–Col Saunders (commanding officer), Sgt J. Thomas (GOC NI Commendation), L/Cpl N. Lloyd (MID), Pte Saunders (GOC NI Commendation), Maj. B. Franklin (MID). Col.-Sgt McIntyre was the second of five brothers who served in the regiment and had already been awarded a GOC NI Commendation in 1981. Lt–Col Saunders, the commanding officer in Hong Kong, had himself been awarded a MID for his work in Northern Ireland in 1981. He was later promoted to brigadier and became the defence attaché in Athens. On 8 June 2000 whilst on the way to work he was murdered by gunmen who belonged to a group called Revolutionary Organisation 17 November (N17).

A group of brothers serving in the battalion, Ballykinler, Northern Ireland, 1974. Again many had family connections with the regiment or its predecessors going back to before the First World War. Left: Hobbs. Centre, front: Kews. Front, right: Tuckers. Second row, second from right: McIntyres. Back row, right: Dowdells. Others are unidentified. The McIntyre brothers, Rory and Stephen, were the third and fourth brothers to serve in the battalion.

Two members of 'C' Company after a hard day's work at the Maze Prison due to the major disturbances of 15 October 1974. Both are wearing the M1952 flak jackets. Pte Finley's headgear is a 1944 pattern steel helmet with face visor fitted. Holding the riot baton is Maj. M. Draper who had many years of experience in situations such as this. As a young officer in the Wiltshire Regiment he was in charge of the search team in Cyprus in 1958 that was responsible for the death of the EOKA second in command, Christoforou Kyriakos Matsis. Maj. Draper took part in the DERR formation parade in 1959, remaining with the battalion for a number of years. He was a battalion sportsman of note, and excelled at cross country running. In 1975 he received commendation of the GOC (NI). He retired in 1980.

Cpl A. Gill, Military Medal, *c.*1975, seen here as the holder of the 'Silver Bugle' presented to the regiment by the old comrades during a visit to the battalion in Berlin 1972. The bugle was inscribed with the regimental crest. Cpl Gill was one of only two Military Medal winners in the regiment, the other being Pte Powell. Cpl Gill was awarded his Military Medal during the so called 'Battle of the Hump' that took place when the Drums Platoon under the command of Drum Major Coveney, reinforced by members of 10 Platoon, was located in 'The Hump' (VCP) overlooking the town of Lifford, near Strabane, 22 February 1974. (See page 95.)

Pte Mark Drummond, 1st Battalion, 1989, showing his newly issued General Service Medal with clasp for Northern Ireland. He was born on 14 August 1969, when soldiers were first committed to Ulster. This General Service Medal was introduced in 1962, and is awarded for at least thirty days of active service. Pte Drummond was a good shot, representing the battalion at Bisley, coming second in the young soldiers' SMG (sterling machine gun) shoot.

Above left: The battalion smallbore team, 1977. From left to right, standing: Cpl Butler, Capt. Holmes, Cpl Patterson, Dmr Wheeler. Sitting: S/Sgt Walls, Capt. Briard, Maj. Martin, Capt. Peters, WO2 Smart. Over a number of years the battalion rifle teams achieved outstanding results at both smallbore and, on occasion, fullbore disciplines. Several members consistently achieved army team status and some were also selected for the combined services team. The driving force was Maj. Peter Martin whose influence and experience extended well beyond regimental and army events, including, in 1990, his selection as captain of the Great Britain team against the United States for the Pershing Trophy. Capt. Holmes was commissioned into the regiment from the Royal Marines bringing with him a valuable expertise in both service and target rifle disciplines. Capt. Peters, after retirement, became the second regimental museum curator, a post he held for thirteen years, becoming an authority on regimental historical matters.

Above right: Lt Chilton (left) briefs Pte Ward, prior to a patrol in Northern Ireland, 1974. Lt Chilton had previously served as a territorial in the 4th/6th Battalion Royal Berkshire Regiment. He served with 1 DERR in British Honduras, Panama, Cyprus and Berlin. He later transferred to the Royal Army Ordnance Corps retiring as a lieutenant colonel after which he became the third regimental museum curator at Salisbury. Pte Ward served for many years. In 1987 he was part of the STANOC (Surveillance, Target Acquisition, Night Observation and Counter-surveillance) team at Larkhill. From there he was deployed as part of the team that conducted a search of the passenger ferry *Herald of Free Enterprise* when it capsized with great loss of life at Zeebrugge. He later remembered:

> There was a group of RN divers there, who I think were part of a training party, but they were searching for survivors. I went with some of them to try and find anyone left alive, as the Spyglass would be able to give an indication of body warmth. Incidentally, the Spyglass worked after immersion, which is more than could be said for me, it was freezing. After a few hours it became clear that there was no-one left alive. I then helped to move bodies out of the ferry, several in some very strange places, I remember a steward who seemed to have locked himself in his wardrobe to get away from the water. It took an hour or so to get his body out. Altogether I assisted with twenty-three bodies, getting them down on to a floating platform next to the wreck. After thirty-six hours we returned home arriving on a Sunday. I flew to Hong Kong to re-join the battalion the following day.

He retired in 1995 as WO2, as RQMS (Tech) of 1 RGBW.

Below left: The commanding officer Lt-Col Jones (left) and WO2 Wiggins deep in conversation with a Royal Engineers explosive team, Londonderry, 1979. A patrol under the command of WO2 Wiggins had spotted a set of car keys, gloves and a hood lying beside the entrance to the cattle market. They maintained observation on these items and later established they belonged to a nearby car that had been reported as hi-jacked. The car was treated as a suspect bomb and the Royal Engineers called out to deal with it. This photograph shows the CO and WO2 Wiggins briefing the operator. The car was eventually cleared and inside some incendiary devices were discovered together with a .45 Webley pistol. Lt-Col Jones had served in the regiment since its formation in 1959. He commanded the battalion from 1977–80. WO2 Wiggins spent most of his career in the battalion. He was an excellent shot, becoming the battalion champion at arms. He excelled at rugby, both playing and coaching. He was later promoted to RSM, taking over 1 Wessex (Rifle Volunteers), followed by a period at the Sennelager training centre in Germany. He was awarded a GOC's commendation for service in NI and later commissioned into the Staffordshire Regiment. After his retirement he was 'recalled' by the regiment, by now 1 RGBW, to coach the battalion rugby team in their quest for the army rugby cup. He was successful with the battalion winning the army cup for the second time.

Below right: L/Cpl David Weaving, 'A' Company, on patrol in the Dundalk Road, Crossmaglen, Northern Ireland, 1984. He was one of three brothers serving in the battalion at that time – Mark was in Bessbrook and Mick in Forkhill. It was common practice in family regiments such as 1 DERR to split up brothers when engaged on active service. L/Cpl Weaving later remembered:

> When that photo was taken we were showing a Dutch Major around our area of responsibility. I was the brick commander [A brick is a four-man team] armed with an Armalite, and the remainder of my patrol were armed with a 'gimpy' [General Purpose Machine Gun], a Bren gun [7.62], an SLR [Self Loading Rifle] plus a 79mm grenade launcher, so all in all we were well armed. At the time we were deployed on a cordon because another patrol has discovered an IED [improvised explosive device] in a nearby lamppost. My brick had gone past the lamppost the day before but fortunately it did not explode because a horse in the field that was next to the lamppost ate the fertilizer that formed part of the explosive, stopping it from going off, I have a soft spot for horses now.

L/Cpl Weaving's regimental cap badge is painted matt black, a practice adopted in Northern Ireland to avoid it becoming an easy target for snipers.

Pte Leighfield, 'D' Company, receiving a commendation from the commander of the British Forces in Hong Kong, Maj.-Gen. Johnson, during the battalion's thirtieth anniversary celebrations, 14 July 1989. Pte Baker also received a commendation. Both were present in the Gurkha barracks in Sek Kong in the New Territories when a grenade exploded in the office of a British officer serving with the Gurkhas. On hearing the explosion they rushed to the scene. They gave immediate first aid to the officer and one other casualty and ensured that they were both evacuated as quickly as possible. Unfortunately the British officer died of his injuries. Both soldiers were awarded the commendation for their quick thinking and prompt action (at the same parade testimonials from the Royal Humane Society were presented to WO2 Maynard and Ptes Harrison and Edwards for saving life at sea).

Lt-Col Kenway unveils the memorial stone at the site of Sandes Soldiers Home where two soldiers, L/Cpl Coughlan and Pte Swanick, were killed by IRA action on 28 October 1974. In addition, during its service in Northern Ireland, the battalion lost a number of soldiers, most of whom are commemorated in the Regimental Book of Remembrance, located in Salisbury Cathedral. Cpl Leahy (8 March 1973); Col.-Sgt Foster (23 March 1973); Capt. Sutton (14 August 1973); Cpl Windsor (6 November 1974); Pte Allen (6 November 1974); Pte Randall (26 June 1993); L/Cpl Pullin (17 July 1993). Many years later after a sustained campaign, comrades of Pte Allen got his name added to the local war memorial in his home town of Ilkeston, Derbyshire. In addition to those who died, there were, of course, numerous soldiers from the battalion who sustained injuries and wounds that led to them being medically discharged.

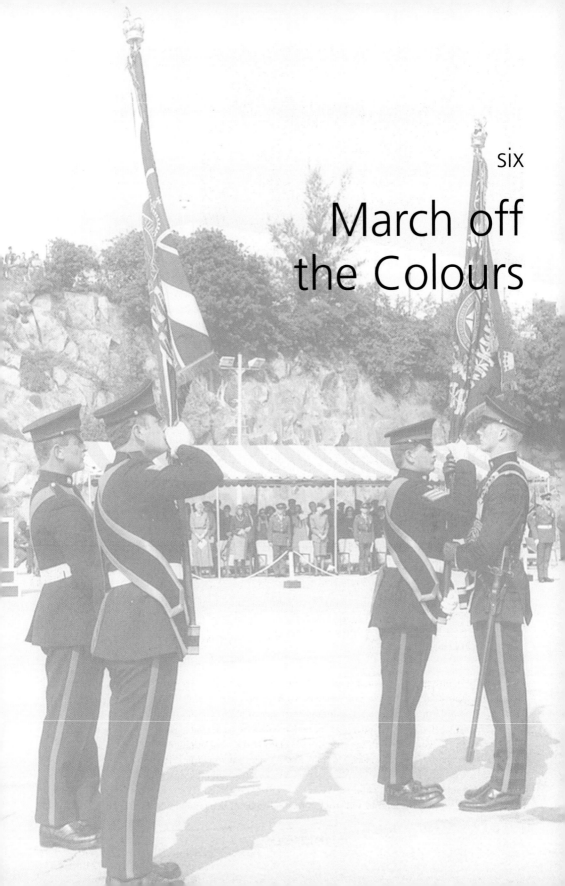

six

March off
the Colours

Above: Queens Birthday Parade, Malta, early 1960s. Sergeants' Colour Party. From left to right: Cpl Turner, Col.-Sgt Whiting (carrying Queen's Colour), Cpl Seward. Col.-Sgt Whiting had previously served in the Coldstream Guards, transferring to the Royal Berkshire Regiment and remaining after the amalgamation into 1 DERR. He shot for a number of years in the battalion smallbore team, and represented the battalion at hockey.

Below: The escort to the Colours march down Kingsway, Valletta, Malta, to take up position for the opening of Parliament, October 1963. In command is Capt. Tremellen, with CSM Briggs as the right guide. In the centre is Pte Pinnell who spent many years in the Regimental Police and later was awarded a British Empire Medal. Capt. Tremellen came to the regiment from the Royal Berkshire Regiment with family connections going back many years. CSM Briggs came to the regiment from the Wiltshire Regiment and was a boxer and coach of some note.

'A' Company, acting as escort to the Colours during the 1967 Ferozeshah Parade in snow-covered Clifton Barracks, Minden, West Germany. From left to right: Maj. Redding, 2nd-Lt Snook, 2nd-Lt Ireson. At the front is Sgt Cross (left guide). All the Ferozeshah parades in Minden took place in the depth of winter with the regiment commemorating the battle as near to 21 December as possible. A soldier who took part in all three parades remembered, 'It was always freezing; I know the battle was fought in the heat of India, but that didn't help us. The spectators were always provided with braziers to keep warm, we were provided with greatcoats, but I can never remember wearing one'.

Drum Major Morris with the Regiment's Colours, Clifton Barracks, Minden, on the tenth anniversary of the formation of the regiment, 1969. (Queen's Colour left, Regimental Colour, right.) At this time the battalion was under the command of Lt-Col Gibson, MBE, who arranged for the whole battalion to be photographed in company groups to commemorate the event. In carrying out this action he was following in the footsteps of the forming regiments (Royal Berkshire and Wiltshire Regiments) who periodically carried out similar exercises over the years in different parts of the world. These photographic records have proved invaluable to regimental historians today. The silver piece on the floor was presented by the Borough of Windsor to commemorate the regiment receiving the freedom of the town in 1960. The silver armoured personnel carrier on the right was commissioned by the officers of the regiment particularly those who served with the 1st Battalion in Minden.

The Regimental Colour being trooped through the ranks of the battalion during the Ferozeshah Parade, Berlin, 23 June 1972. The Colour is being carried by Col.-Sgt Watton. RSM Pinchen (right) commands the escort. This parade was commanded by Lt-Col Crabtree and was watched by 140 former comrades flown over from England. Spectators included ex-Col.-Sgt Crump, who had joined the Royal Berkshires in 1909, and ex-RSM McColm, who went ashore at Normandy on 6 June 1944 with the 5th Battalion. Among many with strong links to the regiment were Mr and Mrs Cook who watched their two sons and one son-in-law, all in the Corps of Drums. It was events such as this that emphasised the link between regiments of the past and the present.

A unique ceremony took place at HMS *Vernon* at Portsmouth when the Colours of 1 DERR were returned from Berlin on HMS *Lewiston* in 1973. The regiment was affiliated to HMS *Vernon*, who provided the escort to the Colours, consisting of two officers and forty-eight ratings. The guard was inspected by Lt-Col W.G.R. Turner, MBE, the commanding officer of the 1st Battalion. Lt Lake (left) is carrying the Queen's Colour and Lt Franklin the Regimental Colour. Between them is Sgt Swift who, several years later, was awarded a Mention in Dispatches for his work in Northern Ireland.

'D' Company under the command of Maj. C Parslow (right), followed by Lt P. King, march through the German town of Osnabrück on the occasion of the freedom of the town being granted to the Garrison, 1980. As was tradition, they marched with Colours flying, bayonets fixed and drums beating. 'D' Company represented the battalion who at this time were in Canada on exercise 'Medicine Man'. The battalion was based in Mercer Barracks as a mechanised infantry battalion within the 12th Armoured Brigade. The L/Cpl to the left in ceremonial uniform is a member of the 5th Royal Inniskilling Dragoon Guards which the battalion was normally grouped for operations.

A sight rarely seen by soldiers from the regiment who never reached the Sergeants' Mess. On the day of a Ferozeshah Parade at the stroke of midnight the Colours would ceremoniously be handed back to the officers. Here we see WO1 (RSM) Venus in 1980 when the battalion was stationed in Osnabrück, West Germany, taking charge of the Regimental Colour prior to handing it back to the officers. The Queen's Colour is being carried at the slope by Col.-Sgt Mortimer, and would be handed over shortly afterwards. The Drum Major who remains at the salute is Drum Major Harrill. This tradition was jealously guarded during the regiment's existence and old comrades from the regiment still meet on 21 December each year in Wiltshire to commemorate this Battle Honour and to honour the men of the 62nd Foot who fought at Ferozeshah.

In April 1962 six Fijian recruits joined the battalion whilst it was serving in Tidworth. They were Ptes Baleimatuku, Ravu, Turaga, Qarau, Conivavalagi and Raidani. Three of these soldiers remained with the battalion for the full term of twenty-two years, playing an active part in both regimental and operational affairs. They particularly excelled at boxing and rugby. Here we see the three remaining soldiers, together with RSM Venus, on their last Ferozeshah Parade in 1983. From left to right: Col.-Sgt Baleimatuku, Sgt Ravu, Col-Sgt Turaga. To mark the end of the Fijians' service both colour sergeants were honoured by being selected to carry the Colours and, as the regimental journal recorded, 'The Commanding Officer could not have entrusted the safe guarding of the Colours to two more loyal and dedicated colour sergeants'.

The battalion marches off the parade square at Osnabrück after the Ferozeshah Parade, 1981. Leading are the assault pioneers wearing white aprons and carrying ceremonial silver axes. From left to right: Cpl Annear, Sgt Rose, Cpl Irving, followed by the commanding officer, Lt-Col Coxon. By tradition, the pioneer sergeants in British army infantry battalions were the only soldiers allowed to wear a beard. The leading of the battalion by the pioneers on ceremonial occasions recalled the times when they had to clear a way across country for the main body of troops to follow.

In 1984 the regiment was given the honour of mounting guard at Buckingham Palace. A company of 150 soldiers together with the Band and Corps of Drums under the command of Maj. Lake came to London for a three-week commitment. In addition to guarding the Palace they mounted guards at the Tower of London and St James's Palace. The commanding officer, Lt-Col Mackereth, who commanded one of the guards, later remembered, 'It was a great feeling marching down the Mall behind one's own regimental band's superb music'. Here we see 2nd-Lt Dennis as he shoulders the battalion's Queen's Colour alongside the Colour of the 1st Battalion Scots Guards on the forecourt of Buckingham Palace.

After being relieved by the Scots Guards, the guard marches out of the forecourt of Buckingham Palace behind the Queen's Colour. In the foreground is Cpl A. McIntyre, the fifth of five brothers to serve in the regiment. When later interviewed for a newspaper he said, 'It's alright, but it gets a bit repetitive, if you like drill, fine, join the Guards, I don't like drill. I'm more your field soldier type'. He later remembered, 'I paid for that comment, as I was relegated to night patrols, well away from the public gaze'. (Cpl McIntyre was later Mentioned in Dispatches for work in Northern Ireland followed by a Queen's commendation for valuable service. He retired as a WO2.)

Shortly before the duty at Buckingham Palace, Field Marshal His Royal Highness Prince Philip, Duke of Edinburgh, the Colonel-in-Chief, had presented new Colours to the regiment at Howe Barracks, Canterbury, on 8 June 1984. The previous stand of Colours had been presented by him in 1959 on the formation of the regiment. The officers receiving the Colours were 2nd-Lts White and Dennis. The escorts for the new Colours were WO2 (CSM) Bryant; Col-Sgts North and McLeod. An old soldier who witnessed the parade and had taken part in many parades in the past said, 'It was a brilliant parade, the lads were very steady and a credit to the regiment. I don't know what it is, but when the Colours appear on parade, with the Battle Honours displayed it gives you real pride'. These Colours were carried until 1994 when they were laid up in the regimental museum after the amalgamation with the Gloucestershire Regiment.

To the strains of 'Auld Lang Syne' the escort to the old Colours slow marches off the parade ground at Howe Barracks, Canterbury, 8 June 1984, after the Colours were trooped through the ranks for the last time. Many present at this parade had witnessed or taken part in the parade twenty-five years previously when the Colours were first presented. The officers carrying the Colours are Lt P. King and 2nd-Lt S. Gray. The escorting NCOs were, from left to right: L/Cpl Owen, Sgt R. Tait, WO2 (CSM) D. Beet (centre) and Sgt G. Bartlett (right). These Colours were later taken to the Regimental Museum at Salisbury before being laid up in the cathedral.

The old Colours are marched from the Wardrobe to Salisbury Cathedral to be laid up on 27 September 1987, with over 700 past and present members of the regiment attending. The Colours were later placed in glass-fronted cases in St Michael's Chapel, joining the regimental Book of Remembrance. Centre of the Colour Party is WO2 Moloney. 'The Wardrobe' in the Cathedral Close was leased to the regimental trustees by the Dean and Chapter for use as a headquarters and museum. Since that time it has developed into one of the finest museums of its kind in the country.

In 1984 the battalion was based in Howe Barracks, Canterbury, Kent. Prior to deploying to Northern Ireland, a family service was held in Canterbury Cathedral on 27 May 1984. Here we see the Colour Party (with the Colours being carried 'at the slope'), headed by Drum Major Tadhunter, as they emerge from the cathedral after the service. The battalion then marched through the city centre, but not with Colours flying and the regimental band playing as the regiment did not have the freedom of the city. There were four companies dressed in combat kit with the drum major, three side drummers and a bass drummer, keeping the beat, all in full ceremonial dress at the centre of the column.

The battalion went to Cyprus in December 1984 for a United Nations tour, remaining for six months. Towards the end of the deployment a representative group from the battalion were presented with their United Nations medals. Here we see the Colour Party under the command of RSM Hicks marching off after the presentation. The medals were presented by the force commander Maj. Gen. Greindl, an Austrian. During the parade the battalion performed an immaculate *feu de joie* accompanied by verses of 'The Farmer's Boy' between the ripples of rifle fire.

Maj.-Gen. Crabtree, CB, the colonel of the Regiment, salutes the Colours during the Ferozeshah Parade in Aldergrove, Northern Ireland, 1987. This was the battalion's final parade with the 7.62 Self Loading Rifle as it was this year that they re-equipped with the new SA 80. Gen. Crabtree was very familiar with the parade

format as he had previously served in the battalion as a company commander, and was also the Commanding Officer 1970–72. He handed over the position of Colonel of the Regiment to Brig. Turner, CBE, in 1988, but due to Brig. Turner's untimely death resumed the appointment in 1989, remaining until 1990. The battalion stayed at Aldergrove until 1988, when it moved to Hong Kong. It returned to the United Kingdom in 1990 for its final tours in Northern Ireland before amalgamation in 1994.

On the 1st Battalion's arrival in Hong Kong the Colours were ceremoniously brought ashore by the Hong Kong patrol craft HMS *Swift*, before being taken to the British Forces Headquarters, Hong Kong, at HMS *Tamar*. The battalion arrived in 1988 on the eve of the Chinese New Year – the year of the dragon. The dragon emblem on HMS *Swift*'s funnel is the insignia of the Hong Kong Squadron. Carrying the Queen's Colour (left) is Lt P. Dennis and Regimental Colour (right) Lt P. Clements. The escort to the rear of this group is Col.-Sgt Tadhunter, who was for a number of years the battalion's drum major. The warrant officer in command of the Colour Party is WO2 McLeod who later in 1992 became the last regimental sergeant major of the 1st Battalion. After amalgamation with the Gloucestershire Regiment he continued serving with 1 RGBW.

Ferozeshah Parade, Stanley Fort, Hong Kong, 14 December 1989. The Commanding Officer Lt-Col D.J.A. Stone delivered the charge in the following terms:

> Warrant Officers and Sergeants of the Duke of Edinburgh's Royal Regiment. I am about to hand over to your custody for a period, the Colours of the 1st Battalion. This high honour is bestowed on you in commemoration of the gallant services rendered by your predecessors at the battle of Ferozeshah, the anniversary of which we celebrate today. Safeguard and honour these Colours as your officers have ever done and let the fact that our Colours are entrusted to your keeping be not only a reminder of past services but also a visible expression of the confidence and trust which to-day your officers justly place in you. Hand over the Colours.

Here we see the officers handing over the Colours that were retained in the Sergeants' Mess until midnight. 2nd-Lt Preece hands the Regimental Colour to Col.-Sgt Stanley. Col.-Sgt Decarteret is already in possession of the Queen's Colour having received it from Lt Flavell. WO2 Maynard remains at the 'present arms' and the two escorts, Sgts Probets and Parks, are just out of picture.

After three years the battalion left Hong Kong, returning to Catterick in the United Kingdom where it became part of 24 Airmobile Brigade. Here we see the Colour Party, ceremoniously marching the Colours onto HMS *Plover*. This represented the start of the return journey back to Britain. The Queen's Colour (right) was carried by Lt Rose, and the Regimental Colour by Lt Delf. In charge of the escort was WO2 Hole. Lt Rose's family had a long association with the regiment, his father having served in the Wiltshire Regiment and 1 DERR. The Colour Party boarded the ship to the haunting strains of 'Auld Lang Syne'. The regimental journal later recorded:

Our thoughts on leaving Hong Kong can be best expressed in the closing lines of our regimental march:

He blessed the day
He came that way
To be a Farmer's Boy, to be a Farmer's Boy...

Ferozeshah Parade, 1990. At this time the battalion was on operations in Northern Ireland as the Fermanagh Roulement Battalion. It was decided that the event should be commemorated, albeit in a revised format, to reflect the operational commitments. Here we see the Colour Parties from the Officers' and Warrant Officers' and Sergeants' Messes. From left to right: Col.-Sgt Williams, Lt Gilchrist (Queen's Colour): Lt Delf (Regimental Colour), Col.-Sgt Sumner. The charge was delivered by the commanding officer and the Colours were handed over to the warrant officers and sergeants. A meal followed for those not deployed with the mess being entertained by a piper from 4 UDR (Ulster Defence Regiment). As was customary the Colours were returned to the officers at midnight.

The Colours during the freedom marches 1991. The battalion exercised its right to the freedom of Wallingford, Abingdon and Chippenham. The colonel of the regiment took the salute at each location alongside the Mayor. These had the effect of raising the profile of the regiment. The regimental

journal reported that the only negative aspect of these events was in Chippenham when Pte Coney bayoneted (accidentally) the OC, resulting in much blood on the Council Chamber floor. From left to right, back row: 2nd-Lt Cooper, WO2 Henwood, Sgt Owen, WO2 Williams, Sgt Wright, Drum Maj. -?-, Sgt Pocock, Col.-Sgt Sumner. Sitting: Lt Griffin, Lt Preece, Maj. Wardle, Lt Baily, Lt O'Hara.

The final parade for the Colours of 1 DERR, (seen here together with the Colours of the Gloucestershire Regiment) as they are marched off at Windsor, 8 June 1994. The DERR Colours were finally laid up in the regimental museum at Salisbury where, preserved in air-tight glass cases, they are currently on display. The Colour Party for this final parade was Lt Ross, Lt Biggs, Sgt-Maj. Truman, Col.-Sgt Wright and Col.-Sgt Stevens. What remained of 1 DERR marched off the parade ground under new Colours as part of the 1st Battalion Royal Gloucestershire, Berkshire and Wiltshire Regiment. Under these new RGBW Colours the soldiers of Berkshire and Wiltshire served in Northern Ireland, the Falklands, Egypt, Kenya, Cyprus, Bosnia, Kosovo and Afghanistan. In 2007 a further amalgamation will occur making the battalion a part of 'The Rifles', and Colours will no longer be carried.

Other titles published by Tempus

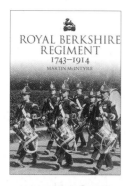

Royal Berkshire Regiment 1743–1914
MARTIN MCINTYRE

The Royal Berkshire Regiment has, from its earliest days, provided the British Army with soldiers committed to defending the nation's interests. Their service to the crown, during the American War of Independence, in the Crimea, Afghanistan, the Boer War, and up to the outbreak of war in 1914 is brought to life in this collection of images.

0 7524 3914 6

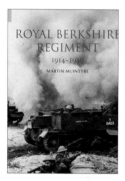

The 2nd Battalion Royal Berkshire Regiment
In World War One

IAN CULL

The 2nd Royal Berkshire Regiment was a fighting force of hardened professionals. Ian Cull traces the action faced by the men of the regiment, and in doing so gives us an insight into trench life and portrays the brutality of the battlefields of Loos and Passchendale with a vividness that gives a sense of the heroism and spirit of the 2nd Royal Berkshire Regiment.

0 7524 3571 X

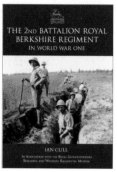

Royal Berkshire Regiment 1914–1959
MARTIN MCINTYRE

Throughout a volatile period in European history the Royal Berkshire Regiment was a bedrock of the British Army. Covering both world wars, Martin McIntyre has traced the modern history of this proud regiment, from the outbreak of war in 1914 to its amalgamation with the Wiltshire Regiment in 1959, with a series of photographs that gives a real sense of military life and the spirit of our soldiers during times of both conflict and peace.

0 7524 3471 3

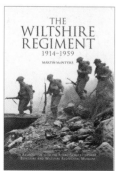

The Wiltshire Regiment 1914–1959
MARTIN MCINTYRE

On the outbreak of war in 1914 the British people reacted with patriotic fervour to the prospect of fighting for King & Country. The Wiltshire Regiment was no exception, and, through a series of photographs portraying regimental life of the time, Martin McIntyre captures a period of great change, from the optimism of the summer of 1914, to the very different reaction on the declaration of war in 1939, to the amalgamation with the Berkshire Regiment in 1959.

0 7524 3757 7

If you are interested in purchasing other books published by Tempus, or in case you have difficulty finding any Tempus books in your local bookshop, you can also place orders directly through our website
www.tempus-publishing.com